Betty Reveley and Allan Wendt

HISTORIC WALKS IN LONDON, BATH, OXFORD & EDINBURGH

Betty Reveley and Allan Wendt

HISTORIC WALKS IN LONDON, BATH, OXFORD & EDINBURGH

W.H. ALLEN · LONDON

Phototypeset by Sunrise Setting, Devon
Printed and bound in Great Britain by
Mackays of Chatham Ltd, Kent
for the Publishers W.H. Allen & Co. PLC
44 Hill Street, London W1X 8LB

ISBN 0 491 03800 3 (W.H. Allen hardcover edition)
ISBN 0 86379 088 7 (Comet Books softcover edition)

Acknowledgements

Illustrations on the following pages are reproduced by permission
of The *Huntingdon Library*, San Marino, California: pp. 11, 23,
27, 29, 45, 46, 57, 72, 80, 83, 85, 111, 115, 121, 124, 127, 138, 142,
143, 146, 148.

Contents

Dedication

To the Master Walkers of London, *Daniel Defoe, Samuel Johnson and John Gay*

Many people have enjoyed walking the streets of London, but Daniel Defoe, Samuel Johnson and John Gay have come close to making a profession out of a pastime. All literary men, they took inspiration from the city that was their home. As eighteenth-century writers, they were central to the postgraduate studies of the two Americans who produced this book. Thus with their writings and example they encouraged the discovery of these walks.

Daniel Defoe, who learned in middle life that he could earn more money making books than making bricks, began by writing stories that came to be called novels — some scholars say he invented the genre. But needing more income than even his popular novels could produce, in 1725 he published an ambitious, multi-volumed description of the whole of Great Britain. Much of it was hackneyed and secondhand, because Defoe was no long-distance traveller, but the section on London, where he had lived all his life, was patently a labour of love. He describes his one-day tour of the city as it was then, roughly the area bounded by the old Roman and Saxon walls, and deplores the creeping suburbanism that he felt was beginning to destroy the surrounding countryside. The beauties of Defoe's compact little city are what we look for in these walks, along with its adjacent villages, which still retain something of their old identity even though they have since been surrounded by urban sprawl.

Samuel Johnson was born in Lichfield, but he came to London when he was twenty-seven years old and he lived in the city and loved it with all the fervour of a convert for the rest of his life. He wrote, 'When a man is tired of London he is tired of life, for there is in London all that life can afford' — lines which might well be an epigraph for this book. He was also an indefatigable walker of London streets — sometimes all night when he was young, for he often did not have the price of a bed. After living a year in the city, Johnson published his first major poem, 'London'. In the popular style of the day, the poem was an imitation of Juvenal, a free adaptation of the Latin writer's comments on ancient Rome. It is satirical but not cynical; only a man who knew and loved his city could point out its spots and patches.

Finally, there was John Gay, best known today for his perennially popular play, *The Beggar's Opera*; he wrote a long poem in 1716 called *Trivia, or The Art of Walking the Streets of London*, which provides epigraphs for most of the walks printed here. John Gay is the genuine master walker to whom we must all serve apprenticeship, for like the writers — and readers — of this book he studied the city and its streets.

He wrote:

> Through London Streets to steer your Course aright,
> How to walk clean by Day, and safe by Night,
> How jostling Crouds, with Prudence, to decline,
> When to assert the Wall, and when resign,
> I sing . . .

9

Preface

How to Use This Book

THIS BOOK should be used not to limit your explorations, but to teach you how to strike out on your own — the walks in this volume barely scratch the surface of possibilities in London, and the several walks in Bath, Oxford and Edinburgh are no more than introductions to these fascinating towns.

The walks here are for your apprenticeship. When you have finished them, or some portion of them, you will become a journeyman or journeywoman, ready and able to explore the inexhaustible treasures of these cities on your own and to discover for yourself all the fascinating experiences that lurk around the next corner or up a nearby lane.

You'll know when you're ready, for your confidence will increase as your curiosity grows, not only about what is in these pages but more importantly about what is not. When you find yourself turning aside impatiently from the recommended directions, when you begin to find more interesting things than those described on these pages, when you finally start out one morning and realize that you have forgotten this book but continue anyway — these are sure signs that your apprenticeship is coming to an end.

We should say too, at the outset, that these walks are for serious walkers, those who suffer from chronic tourist's indigestion from too many half-day bus tours to a dozen different monuments, from too many three-week tours

through ten different countries. Serious but not solemn walkers, for one finds much satisfaction in exploring beneath the surface of things and much entertainment in discovering aspects of the city that even the natives don't know. Serious but not scholarly walkers, for although there is much history along these walks, it is primarily visual, to be found in buildings, streets, gardens, statues, lamp-posts, pictures and decorations. We try to help you see what still is, not what used to be; looking at a block of office buildings that used to be the site of a famous old coaching inn can be singularly unentertaining.

Serious walkers, finally, who will want a record of their achievements. For this reason we recommend keeping a journal of your explorations, a daily account of places visited and new things seen. Otherwise all those individual chunks of experience may get lost; all that will remain will be an amorphous mass of indistinguishable memories. You may even have trouble identifying the pictures you took

11

with such care at the time. A journal need not be a work of literary art, but it will be a great pleasure to the writer in the years to come.

Clearly, no single book can say all that needs saying about these cities, particularly about London. Most obvious omissions are the places that everyone knows about — Westminster Abbey, the Tower of London and the British Museum. It is easy to learn about them; this book looks for the unexpected and the lesser known sights. And, as an apprenticeship course, this book tries to stimulate your desire to explore, not to satiate it. There are certainly dozens more walks in London, Bath, Oxford and Edinburgh that are just as interesting as these. Our choices are frankly arbitrary and personal.

Even on the walks outlined here there are many things to see that are not described. That is part of the pleasure of walking and part of the reason for keeping a journal. The book chiefly aims at making your exploration easy. We begin, for this reason, with a brief chapter on the walker's 'tools' — principally London public transport, a system that will get you where you want to go and back again as quickly, as efficiently and as cheerfully as any transport system in the world. But for the first-time user, the system has its mysteries as well; this chapter will advise, guide, warn.

Following this, the first walk is designed to introduce the apprentice to three geographical 'centres' of London. For such a large city, London can be surprisingly small; these three centres — one in Westminster, one in the City, and one, historically at least, in between, will enable the walker to take bearings and to keep from ever being hopelessly lost.

Following this, the order of the London walks should depend entirely on each walker. Together they cover large parts of central London, with special expeditions to Hampstead, Hammersmith, Kew Gardens and Greenwich. Individually, they may appeal to a wide range of interest; they should accordingly be picked for that appeal. In the book, the walks simply begin in the centre of things and radiate outwards.

Similarly, the walks in the other cities do not attempt to be comprehensive, but clearly it is easier to cover large portions of Oxford and Bath and even Edinburgh in a couple of days' walking than it is to cover the great mass of London.

Actual walking distances are not great, usually two miles or less, but most walkers will probably extend that with side trips, and everyone will need to save some energy for that peculiarly wearing 'museum shuffle', the hesitant gait of visitors inside important buildings. Most trips are planned to take half a day, but late opening times of many museums and galleries (usually 10 a.m. on weekdays, 2 p.m. on Sundays), along with the need to avoid commuting hours on public transport, would suggest beginning in the mid-morning and finishing by mid-afternoon.

Most important, the walks described here are designed not to constrain but to encourage: when the book says turn right and your desires say turn left, you must learn to have the courage of your inclinations. For that matter, if the directions become so confusing that you seem lost, consider it a reward rather than a punishment as you continue to explore on your own. The real joy of walking is that you will not exhaust that joy after fifteen walks or even fifty. Once you become a journeyperson, this book will be useless, for you will create your own itineraries. Our aim here is to make ourselves redundant.

Cities change, so by the time you take these walks you will surely discover errors, omissions, perhaps additions. Will you write to us, care of the Publishers, about any of these things? We would like to hear from you.

Betty Reveley and Allan Wendt

Tools of the Walker's Trade

What Walker shall his mean Ambition fix,
On the false Lustre of a Coach and Six? . . .
O rather give me sweet Content on Foot,
Wrapt in my Vertue, and a good *Surtout*!

John Gay

BEFORE YOU begin your walking apprenticeship, you need
to provide yourself with a few essential tools: we'll describe
here some things you need for London, since most of these
walks are in London, but many of the suggestions apply to
any new city that you are exploring the first time. Perhaps
most important, and so obvious as to scarcely merit
mention, the walker needs — in addition to virtue and a
'good Surtout' or coat — a good pair of shoes: solidly built,
with low heels and good arch supports, the kind of shoes
that are bought for service rather than style. Nothing can
spoil a pleasant walk more quickly than a blister on the heel;
be sure to have at least one pair of well-broken-in, stout
walking shoes in your luggage before you leave home.

For London, then, besides shoes, you need a good city
map, with a street index, a bus and Underground map, and
probably a weekly bus and Underground pass for the
Central Zone. An hotel will probably supply an
Underground map free, as well as a simple tourist map of
London. But for serious walking you will need something
better: the *A–Z* map, available at most bookshops and
magazine stands, is a good and popular choice. It is clearly
printed, has a comprehensive street index and
Underground map, as well as outline maps showing the
location of important theatres and cinemas. There are a
range of *A–Z* publications; be sure you get the folding map
of central London.

14

The bus and Underground pass is optional, but strongly recommended. If you take at least two short trips a day, it will save you money and it will save you even more time and frustration standing in a queue for Underground tickets or fumbling for change on a moving bus. To obtain a pass you will need a passport-sized picture; if you don't have one with you, stop at the photo machines located in most Underground stations. They will provide you with four pictures in just about as many minutes.

Take the pictures to an Underground ticket office and ask for a one-week Central Zone bus and Underground pass; the ticket seller will provide you with a neat plastic folder showing your picture on one side and your dated pass on the other. Try to order your pass at midday, not during busy rush hours, in order to avoid holding up the queue of ticket buyers. Alternatively you can obtain it at one of the special windows in a few central stations like Piccadilly.

This Central Zone pass will take you on all buses and Underground trains in central London, roughly the area bounded by the Circle Underground line. A more accurate zone description is shown on maps in Underground stations and on printed bus maps. If you travel outside the Central Zone, you will have to pay extra, but you should still use the pass because it will save you part of the fare. The pass is valid until midnight on the sixth day after it is issued; if you buy it on Monday it will be valid until the following Sunday at midnight.

Thus prepared for public transport, you are ready for a few words of instruction about the Underground and bus systems. The Underground is simpler, and is therefore most often used by tourists, but the bus is far more rewarding, if slower. On the Underground, all you have to do is to plot your course on a map and follow the signs. If you have a pass, you simply show it to the ticket collector every time you enter or exit from a station. If you are buying a ticket, you get it at the ticket window or from one of the automatic machines, paying according to distance. Show it to the ticket collector as you enter, or put it in the ticket machine in some stations, and give it up to a ticket collector as you leave the station at your destination.

For most journeys in central London, you simply get on whatever train appears on the platform to which the signs have led you. The exception is the platforms of the Circle line, which is also the only line that goes around continuously (in both directions) instead of from point to point. The Circle line shares tracks with both the District and Metropolitan lines, but you can tell which train has arrived by the sign on the front of the train and by the electric indicators on the platform. Sometimes you may take either train to your destination. If you should find yourself on the wrong train, don't worry — nothing will be lost except time. Just get off at the next station and recalculate your route.

London buses provide more of a challenge to the tourist, but if you find yourself in trouble you may take consolation from knowing that London buses provide challenges even to Londoners. It's part of the game. The first question is, of course: What bus do I take?

London Transport has provided a free map that is a great help. You can get one at any of the Travel Information Centres scattered about London; we'll pass one on our first walk. The bus map gives you a lot more information than we can summarize here, but, most important, it shows all the principal intersections in central London, with a circle at each intersection containing the numbers of the buses that pass there. You simply look at where you are, and where you want to be, and find a number that appears in both places — that's your bus. If there isn't one, you will need to find an intermediate point and make a change. This will require two fares (or a pass); there are no 'transfers' in London.

The next problem is to find a place to get on the bus you want. London buses do not stop at every corner; in fact they rarely stop at intersections. Most important, not all buses on a single street stop at the same place; you need to find a bus stop that includes the number of your bus. At complicated intersections like Marble Arch and Trafalgar Square this can be difficult. There will usually be maps displayed in various places, including the Underground stations, that show where the bus stops are. Eventually, of course, you will remember the stops you use most frequently, and learn also how to locate bus stops you have never used before. It's more of an art than a science.

The final problem with buses is knowing when to get off. On the Underground this is easy, because each station has its name emblazoned boldly at regular intervals along the wall; also maps in each carriage help you anticipate your arrival. No such help is available on buses or at stops. You may know that you want to get off at Oxford Circus, but until you learn to recognize that intersection, and until you learn the location of the nearest bus stop, you will need to rely on the bus conductor. If you are buying a ticket you will need to tell her (more likely than him) where you are going anyway, and you can ask her to call out the stop. Bus conductors' behaviour ranges from helpful to downright surly, but they will always give this minimal assistance. When you ask, speak loud enough so that nearby passengers hear; they will make it their personal responsibility to see that you get off at the right place.

Finally, a brief word about London taxis, which are the easiest method of transport to use but of course the most expensive — although London taxis may well be cheaper than taxis in most large cities. With three or four people sharing the fare, in fact, they hardly cost more than the bus.

London taxis used to be black and box-like, but they have recently blossomed into a rainbow of colours, sometimes with advertising signs on the doors. But they are still box-like, which is a promise of interior comfort and plenty of leg room — the space is supposed to be adequate even if you're a tall man wearing a top hat. You can recognize them by their shape and by the light on the roof showing availability, along with the lighted 'For Hire' sign behind the driver.

All standard taxis are metered, but there is a small additional charge for extra passengers or luggage stowed beside the driver. The driver will also expect at least a 10 per cent tip, perhaps 15 per cent if you are feeling generous. He (still almost always 'he') will be knowledgeable and courteous, for he has to pass a difficult test to get his licence and complaints could cause him to lose it. You may trust him to take you where you want to go by the shortest and most direct route.

He will also rescue you when all else falls — you will see many hands go up for taxis in the bus queue when no bus has appeared for fifteen minutes. At the same time, as in all big cities, taxis mysteriously disappear when the rain fails, or late at night, after a post-theatre supper. Very late at night can be a difficult time for public transport. A few special buses run all night, but infrequently, and the Underground shuts down soon after midnight. So it is best to play Cinderella and get home before your coach turns to a pumpkin.

But this is enough theory. Time now for the practical part of this apprenticeship: your first walk.

Piccadilly

Walk 1   *Westminster, Bank*   ³/₄ mile

> . . . Thou *Trivia,* Goddess, aid my Song,
> Thro' spacious Streets conduct thy Bard along;
> By thee transported, I securely stray
> Where winding Alleys lead the doubtful Way,
> The silent Court, and op'ning Square explore,
> And long perplexing Lanes untrod before.
>
> *John Gay*

THE PURPOSE of this walk is to become familiar with three
means of public transport — Underground, bus and boat —
and to acquaint you with three of London's principal
'centres'. We've discussed public transport in the last
chapter; now it's time to take maps and pass in hand and try
a practical application. Even if your shoes are new and
untried on the pavements, you needn't worry, for this is
more of a ride than a real 'walk'.

First, then, proceed to our starting point, the first centre,
Piccadilly Circus, a location so well known to visitors that it
is almost synonymous with central London. You can get to
Piccadilly Circus easily by bus or Underground — only a
coward would take a taxi. There are two Underground
lines, Piccadilly and Bakerloo, and no fewer than sixteen
bus routes, which we'll list here because you may not yet
have your bus map: Nos. 3, 6, 9, 12, 13, 14, 15, 19, 22, 23, 38,
53, 55, 88, 100, 159.

If you choose to travel by Underground, go to the nearest
station and plan your route. If either the Piccadilly or

19

Bakerloo line runs through your station you should have no trouble — just make sure you travel in the right direction. If neither does, find the shortest route, with the fewest changes, and remember the name of the station where you make the change. From there on it's just a matter of following the signs.

If you are taking the bus, go to the first bus stop you can find and see if one or more of the numbers listed above appears there. And then, of course, make sure you are travelling in the right direction, because these buses also come *from* Piccadilly. Ask someone by the bus stop or ask the conductor as soon as you get on. And don't be embarrassed if you have to cross the street and wait for one coming from the other direction. If you don't find one of those numbers, you will either have to find another bus stop or a place to change; if you don't yet have a bus map, any conductor will give advice. So will other people waiting at the stop.

You should have no trouble recognizing Piccadilly Circus — you've probably seen photographs of it. There are lots of large buildings with glittering advertising signs, almost solid traffic revolving slowly around the circle, and in the middle, poised delicately on one foot, the familiar statue of the Angel of Charity, more often called 'Eros' by the generations of young people who cluster around his feet every summer. The statue was erected in honour of the great nineteenth-century philanthropist, the Earl of Shaftesbury, and his pose constitutes a pun. If you look closely, you will see that he is holding his bow and arrow in such a way that he is about to 'bury' the 'shaft' in the ground, hence 'Shaftesbury'.

Piccadilly Circus is now the geographical heart of London, as we shall see in a moment when we examine its relationship to the rest of the city; but when it was first built up around 300 years ago it was important as a crossroads equidistant from the commercial 'City' to the east and the royal enclave of Westminster to the south. 'Circus' merely means a traffic 'circle', and the curious word 'Piccadilly' comes from one of the first builders here, a tailor who made his money manufacturing starched ruffs or collars, called 'piccadillies'. When he built his house here in the early seventeenth century, he found himself living in the country (hard to believe when you look around today), but within an easy coach ride of his commercial interests in the 'City'.

We'll begin our investigation of Piccadilly Circus underground. If you came by train you will know how to get back down; if you came by bus you need to find one of the nine stairways leading down. The Underground station here is one of the largest in London, a complete circle full of shops, restaurants, bars and other services, as well as ticket machines and ticket offices for the Underground, of course. You might like to walk around first just to familiarize yourself with what is available: note some of the large wall maps of the area and the signs at each exit which provide information about what is above ground. Make sure you stop at the Travel Information Centre to get a central London bus map and a good Underground map. They also have other free printed information.

When you're ready to return above ground, take Subway 2 and follow the signs to Eros Island. The Eros Island exit will actually bring you up on the north side of Regent Street and you will still have to negotiate a short street crossing to the island. You will be well advised to wait until the traffic light is in your favour, for English vehicular traffic shows little concern for pedestrians. And, for visitors who come from other parts of the world, the English custom of driving on the left-hand side of the road can also present a hazard; you should always pay careful attention to the signs that are painted on the street at intersections: 'Look Right', or, occasionally, 'Look Left'. Whenever you can, use the zebra crossings, broad white stripes painted on the road and marked by yellow flashing lights at each end, which indicate right of way to pedestrians.

Once safely on Eros Island, you might like to walk around the base of the statue to familiarize yourself with the five principal thoroughfares that radiate from here. A look at your map will help you. The street names appear high on the buildings; and you can get a compass bearing by realizing that the Angel of Charity is aiming his arrow south-west. Piccadilly is just to the right of his aim.

The street known as Piccadilly leads to an area of wealth and prestige. To the left of the street is the area called St James's, which includes St James's Palace, a former royal residence, and a little further on, through Green Park, Buckingham Palace, the present royal residence. We will follow this route on Walk No. 5. Walking up Piccadilly, to the right is Mayfair and then one reaches the green expanse of Hyde Park; some of London's finest hotels face the park from Mayfair, but the Ritz is on Piccadilly, just before Green Park.

Now move clockwise around Eros Island and you will see the beginning of a great curved avenue lined with impressive buildings with splendid arches. This is Regent Street, north, named after the Prince Regent in the early nineteenth century and designed by the architect Nash to connect Regent's Park in the north with the Prince Regent's mansion at Carlton House. Today Regent Street is an expensive shopping street, which leads in about half a mile to Oxford Circus.

Another clockwise turn around Eros, bypassing the small Glasshouse Street, and you will come to Shaftesbury Avenue, a little shabby now, but leading north-west to many important theatres and cinemas. And the next street is the eastern extension of Piccadilly, which soon becomes Coventry Street and leads to Leicester Square, another rather down-at-heel entertainment area, but one that contains the half-price ticket booth, a place that eventually attracts every London visitor, as well as Londoners themselves, in search of a bargain. Most West End theatres offer unsold tickets there at half price on the day of performance, which makes it well worth standing in a queue.

Once more clockwise and you should be able to identify, off the tip of Eros Island, the beginnings of Haymarket going south, chiefly by the many cars and buses that sweep around the circus and disappear down it. Like many streets in London, its name betrays its earlier function, but today it includes fine shops, theatres and cinemas. It leads in a very short distance to another well-known place, Trafalgar Square, with Lord Nelson's Column, the National Gallery,

Charing Cross, as well as a great number of pigeons. We will explore the square in Walk No. 2.

Finally, the last street on the circuit is the southern extension of Regent Street. It leads to Waterloo Place and the Mall and finally to the government offices in Whitehall and Westminster Square, as well as the Houses of Parliament and Westminster Abbey; in short, to the second important 'centre' we shall visit today. The tall column in the centre of Waterloo Place is the Duke of York's Column; beyond, you should be able to catch a glimpse of the Victoria Tower of the parliament buildings.

To catch a bus for Westminster, you will have to walk over to Haymarket, which runs one way south, whereas lower Regent Street runs one way north. The buses you want stop at the first stop down Haymarket; you can take whichever comes first: the 3, the 88, or the 159.

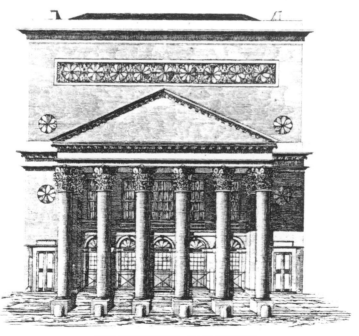

THEATRE ROYAL, HAYMARKET

Any of these buses will take you as quickly as traffic allows down the short stretch of Haymarket, left at the bottom of Trafalgar Square, past the imposing façade of the National Gallery, the historic church of St Martin-in-the-Fields, past Lord Nelson on top of his pillar surrounded by the four crouching lions at its base; it will finally swing down Whitehall to Parliament Square.

This is another area that all visitors will recognize, but if you are at all in doubt, ask the conductor when you show your pass or buy your ticket to let you know when to get off. The bus should stop just before the square. We will have a quick walk around before going on to the third and last centre.

When you get to the corner first look left, or east, to the river and Westminster Bridge. This is where Wordsworth imagined himself standing as he composed the famous sonnet which begins, 'Earth has not anything to show more fair . . .'—thousands of tourists have agreed with him. On the way to the bridge, on the right, is another familiar sight — Big Ben, more properly the name of the bell (named after Sir Benjamin Hall, First Commissioner of Works when it was first hung), but generally applied to the clock tower itself.

The clock tower is part of the elaborate and fascinating neo-Gothic Houses of Parliament, built in the nineteenth century. As you walk along the eastern edge of Parliament Square, you will perhaps notice a queue of people waiting to get in to witness the parliamentary debates — if parliament is in session. The huge building closest to the pavement as you proceed is Westminster Hall, built at the end of the fourteenth century; it is the only survivor from the much older palace that once stood in this area.

If you continue your walk in this direction you will be following the river, past Victoria Tower Gardens and eventually to one of London's most important art galleries, the Tate. Now, however, cross over Margaret Street at the southern end of the square and you will be confronted by Westminster Abbey.

In your admiration for the abbey, be sure not to miss the smaller St Margaret's Church on the corner, built in the late fifteenth century and still the official church of the House of Commons. Westminster Abbey of course deserves a separate visit; as this is simply an orientation walk and we still have ground to cover, for now we will pass by with merely a glance at the exterior.

At the south-west corner of the square, Broad Sanctuary leads south-west to Victoria Street and soon to Victoria Station, an important rail and bus terminal. Walk up to the north-west corner of the square and you will see Great George Street leading west, soon to become Birdcage Walk, which runs along St James's Park and leads eventually to Buckingham Palace.

And as you walk around the square, don't forget to look at the many monuments and statues which seem to fill the area, the eminent statesmen whose voices at one time echoed in the parliament chambers nearby. But we are also in royal London — the kings and queens of England have lived in this area for hundreds of years: in Westminster Palace, Whitehall Palace, St James's Palace and now Buckingham Palace. And the noblemen of the court built their houses nearby, in St James's, in Mayfair, and in the area to the south and west of Parliament Square.

But if the king and his nobles lived and ruled in Westminster, the economic affairs of the nation, after the seventeenth century, were controlled several miles to the north and east by the middle-class bankers and merchants. Their role gradually became more important as the country's well-being came to depend on trade rather than on armed conquest. And it is to the 'City' of London that we must now turn.

To get there we'll try an older and more leisurely form of transport — a boat. Long before good roads were built, the Thames was the principal avenue for travel in and about the city, and long before many bridges spanned the river, small boats were as numerous as present-day taxis and equally quick to come to your call. Every street that came down to the river had a set of 'water steps' to make such travel easy; many public buildings as well as private residences were built with arching 'water gates' that allowed visitors to dock comfortably inside. As you ride a comfortable cabin cruiser down river you should be able to see vestiges of those steps and archways, although some are now well back from the river's edge, for the course of the Thames is now controlled by a man-made embankment that was constructed in the nineteenth century.

To catch the boat you must proceed to Westminster Pier, down some steps to your left just as you start to cross Westminster Bridge. Alternatively you can reach the pier via a subway that connects it to the Underground station. Once you arrive you will see a number of small booths offering rides both up and down the river. Later you may want to try one of the longer trips, up to Kew Gardens, or down to Greenwich or the Thames Barrier, but today you should buy a 'single' ticket (meaning one way, as opposed to a 'return' meaning both ways) to the Tower of London. The ticket seller will point out where to board the boat. In summertime you will probably ride on an excursion boat, with the pilot pointing out interesting sights along the way. But it is helpful for orientation purposes to follow your route on the map.

You will pass under seven bridges. The first is a train bridge leading to Charing Cross railway station on the north bank. It is also a foot bridge, the Hungerford, which will lead the walker to the massive entertainment complex on the south bank that includes the Royal Festival Hall, the National Film Theatre and the National Theatre. Very soon after, just as the river curves around to the right, you will go under Waterloo Bridge, leading to Waterloo railway station on the south bank.

Next comes Blackfriars Bridge. By this time you are well within the 'City' and should be able to see the great City landmark, St Paul's Cathedral, on the north bank. Standing on a hill, it still manages to dominate the skyline as its architect, Christopher Wren, intended, despite the recently erected skyscrapers now surrounding it.

There is another railway bridge after Blackfriars, then comes Southwark Bridge, which leads to the Borough of Southwark on the south bank, where Shakespeare's Globe Theatre originally stood, then another railway bridge and finally London Bridge; there has been a bridge at this point

26

TOWER OF LONDON

across the Thames since Roman times.

The present London Bridge is very new; it was completed in 1973. The old bridge was dismantled piece by piece and shipped to Havasu City, Arizona, where it is reported that its buyer was disappointed with its plainness — it is believed that he thought he had bought the far more distinctive Tower Bridge.

Or perhaps he thought he had bought the original London Bridge, which had houses and shops right along its length and a series of closely spaced piers, so that 'running the bridge' in a small boat could be very dangerous, particularly when the tide was going out. Most passengers heading downstream disembarked above the bridge, walked around and took another boat on the downstream side.

But our boat will slip between the widely spaced piers of the modern bridge with no difficulty. Just beforehand, you should be able to see, on the south side, the towers of Southwark Cathedral, one of the oldest church buildings in

London. Immediately after London Bridge, to the north, between the tall office buildings you should be able to catch a glimpse of the slender tower that is the Monument to the Great Fire of London which burned most of the City in 1666.

Shortly after, you should see the impressive outline of Tower Bridge, with its centre span that can be drawn up to allow large ships to pass beneath, and the Tower of London itself, another London landmark recognizable even to people who have never visited the city. If you look closely at the waterfront in front of the Tower, you will see an arched water gate, where prisoners destined for the Tower would be brought by boat in the middle of the night.

The boat will be docking at Tower Pier. You could visit the Tower now if you wish, but it really deserves a day or at least a half-day to itself. It would be better to admire it from the outside as you walk straight out from the pier and up Tower Hill. You are now at the eastern boundary of the City of London, the terminus of the original Roman wall. At the top of the hill, near the Underground station, you can see excavated remnants of that wall, as well as the medieval one which was added to it.

Our walk today will take us west once more, into the centre of the City. Using your map, start from the top of Tower Hill and set off in a slightly zigzag manner along Byward Street, Great Tower Street and Eastcheap. Here you will see much evidence of the City's concern with business, both in the small and narrow streets that represent the growth of a commercial area and in the many new, large office buildings that continue to be built here.

At the western end of Eastcheap, cross the busy intersection and take King William Street, running diagonally to the north-west. King William Street joins Lombard Street just before it enters the major intersection that is the destination of today's walk; if you proceed on the right-hand side of Lombard Street you will find yourself standing beside two Underground exits — this is a good viewing spot.

Appropriately, the Underground station and the area itself are called 'Bank'. Here you are surrounded by buildings that control the financial affairs of the nation and

MANSION HOUSE

29

to some extent the world. To the right, behind the triangular area containing an equestrian statue of the Duke of Wellington, is the Royal Exchange, with its massive columns and Corinthian pediment. The real stock market is now down the road, but this building still functions as a symbol of financial power.

Looking left, the great concrete building is the Bank of England, the central bank of the country, the government's bank, the issuer of British bank notes. Left again, another bank and then, with its columns and pediment that seem to reflect those of the Royal Exchange, is Mansion House, the ceremonial residence of the Lord Mayor of London.

The Lord Mayor once wielded considerable power; even the monarch had to ask the Lord Mayor's permission before travelling through the City. Today the office has little political significance, but when the new Lord Mayor rides in November to the Lord Mayor's Show in his (or recently, her) gilded coach, the pomp and circumstance rival that of the royal family itself.

From this central point, the City spreads in all directions. To the north lies the great arts centre, the Barbican, the London home of the Royal Shakespeare Company. To the east, the direction from which we came, lie new and old office buildings as well as the Tower. To the south is the river with its great wharves and warehouses, including Billingsgate Fish Market, now moved further downstream, since large vessels no longer come this far up the river. A hundred years ago or so, this was the busy centre of England's world trade.

To the west, up Poultry and Cheapside (which we'll explore in Walk No. 13), is a maze of small streets whose names reflect their former tenants: Poultry itself, Milk Street, Bread Street, Oat Lane and the great Smithfield wholesale meat market, formerly a place where cattle and horses were brought for sale. In this area you may also find many of the guild halls, representing the various trades that were practised in the City.

Finally, a little south of west is St Paul's, the City cathedral, as opposed to the royal Abbey of Westminster. When the present Prince of Wales chose to be married in St

Paul's, his decision not only broke tradition, but bound together two quite different and in many respects opposing areas of the capital city.

This is the end of our first exploratory walk, which, it is hoped, has stimulated you to explore these areas further. If you spend a few minutes later with your map, retracing the route we have taken today, you will realize that we have identified some of the great landmark locations.

Getting home should be easy too, wherever you are staying. There is an Underground station at Bank serving both Northern and Central lines, with an escalator link to Monument station, which will provide access to the Circle and District lines, as well as access to a special short line that will take you direct to Waterloo underground station. You should therefore be able to get anywhere in central London with no more than one change. Just follow the signs.

There are many buses at Bank, too, if you prefer this means of transport; use your bus guide to pick one going your way. You know the rules now, so you should be able to find your way and move anywhere by public transport with confidence. Having travelled west, east, and centre along the axis of the Thames, you need never fear getting lost. The first stage of your apprenticeship is over and London beckons.

Charing Cross,
National Portrait Gallery   ¹/₄ mile

Has not wise Nature strung the Legs and Feet
With firmest nerves, design'd to walk the Street?

John Gay

THIS COULD well be an early walk, taken while you are still
getting oriented to London, for it examines an important
junction between the City to the east and Westminster to
the west and south. It will also serve as an introduction to
some London characters, since these expeditions are
intended to introduce the people who have walked these
streets before you, famous and infamous, well known and
obscure, artists, writers, politicians and princes.

Getting to Charing Cross is easy: almost all central
London buses pass here and there is an Underground
station as well. Or you could easily walk south from either
Piccadilly Circus or Leicester Square. Charing Cross, the
southern end of Trafalgar Square, is a very ancient road
junction, linking one of the principal routes between town
and Crown. The cross itself that gives the place its name
stands in front of the railway station entrance. It is a replica
of the original put there in 1291 by Edward I to mark the last
of thirteen stages in the funeral procession of his wife
Eleanor to Westminster Abbey.

TRAFALGAR SQUARE

But the most famous monument in this area is, of course, Nelson's Column, 185 feet high, erected in 1841 to honour the victor of the Battle of Trafalgar. A monumental statue of Nelson stands on top and four huge lions surround the base — a place where children (and adults) love to have their pictures taken. Also memorable, of course, are the pigeons and the tourists who feed them.

Perhaps the best way to get to know the area is to walk around the square, crossing the roads carefully, for here is some of the heaviest traffic in all of London. The busy thoroughfare to the east is the Strand, a street of hotels, theatres and shops; in a short distance, when it crosses the boundary into the City, it becomes Fleet Street, famous for its newspaper offices. This broad street leads to the heart of middle-class economic power, the City.

To the south-west, through Admiralty Arch, lies the Mall, the direct route to Buckingham Palace and royal London. South runs Whitehall, which leads past government buildings to Parliament Square, with Big Ben, the Houses of Parliament and Westminster Abbey. These are the roads to political power.

At the top of Whitehall stands an equestrian statue to remind us of the frequent historical clash between these powerful interests. Charles I looks down the road to the spot where he was beheaded in 1642, in front of his Banqueting House, which still stands and is open to visitors. Charing Cross is also the scene of the triumphant return of Charles's son, Charles II, at the Restoration in 1660 and, in the same year, of the execution of eight of the regicides who had voted for the execution of Charles I. Samuel Pepys later wrote in his diary: 'Thus it was my chance to see the King beheaded at Whitehall and to see the first blood shed in revenge for the blood of the King at Charing Cross.' Here, too, a pillory was situated for the milder punishment of those who criticized the power structure; Daniel Defoe, the author of anti-government pamphlets, was so honoured.

Moving now to the northern half of Trafalgar Square, you will see Cockspur Street and Pall Mall East, both of which converge in a short block at Haymarket, which in turn leads north to Piccadilly Circus. For the purpose of catching buses, however, you should also look at a map to note that Regent Street runs parallel to Haymarket to the west and that each of these broad avenues carries one-way traffic, Regent Street to the north, Haymarket to the south. Nevertheless bus stops are still always on the left-hand side of the street.

From the north-east corner of the square, Charing Cross Road leads north, first to Leicester Square and then to Oxford Street. St Martin's Lane also runs north and both these thoroughfares lead through the heart of the West End theatre district.

But our attention will now centre on some of the monumental buildings on the north side of Trafalgar Square. The National Gallery, with its massive columns and splendid porch, looms over the square from the north; the church of St Martin-in-the-Fields is just to the right as you face the National Gallery; and the National Portrait Gallery, the final goal of this walk, cannot be seen from the square; it lies behind the National Gallery and is entered from St Martin's Lane.

The National Gallery, as the name suggests, is subsidized by the government and houses an impressive representation of Western European art. Because the collection is so comprehensive, it is difficult to view in a single visit; when you go, it is best to choose to concentrate on a particular period, or a particular painter. The collection is arranged chronologically and there are excellent printed guides available. There are very few paintings by English painters here; the national collection of English art is housed in the Tate Gallery (see Walk No. 6). One other tip: if you find the main entrance to the National Gallery crowded, as you often will in summer, you can walk round to the rear entrance on Orange Street—you will avoid the crush.

The best view of St Martin-in-the-Fields is from the porch of the National Gallery. There you will be able to savour the unusual combination of a classical portico with a medieval steeple. This was the invention of James Gibbs, one of Christopher Wren's pupils, who built the church in 1722. The design has since been copied — not always successfully — in countless churches, including many small wooden American churches in New England.

You may like to walk inside the church. It has a splendid decorated ceiling and a very old pulpit and font. You may also visit the crypt, which was once a burial vault but is now used for social events after services. Charles II was christened here; one of his favourite mistresses, Nell Gwynn, is buried here.

We'll move now to the National Portrait Gallery. This gallery is primarily concerned with English history; it exhibits nearly 10,000 paintings, sculptures and drawings of men and women who have made significant contributions to national life. Not all the portraits have equal artistic value, but many are by some of England's greatest painters, including Reynolds, Gainsborough and Hogarth.

The collection is arranged chronologically and you would do well to pick up a printed guide before you begin your tour. The portraits begin with Henry VII and Henry VIII and his wives and continue with all the monarchs up to the present. You can see Charles I, whose statue we saw looking down Whitehall, and his son, Charles II, who is represented by one full-length portrait. You will see many of Charles's mistresses, the Duchess of Portsmouth, the Duchess of Cleveland and plain Nell Gwynn.

Then there are portraits of Charles's successors to the throne: his brother, James II, who ruled so briefly, William and Mary, Queen Anne, whose many children all died young, and the series of Georges. You will see as well all the great early writers — John Milton, John Dryden, John Bunyan, Thomas Hobbes and Sir Isaac Newton — and later the eighteenth-century men and women: Jonathan Swift, Alexander Pope, Samuel Richardson, Henry Fielding, Fanny Burney and Samuel Johnson. There's a portrait of the great actor David Garrick and a remarkably lifelike painted wooden bust of his contemporary, actor, playwright and theatre manager, Colley Cibber.

Generals, politicians, scientists, historians, musicians and the painters themselves, the latter often in self-portraits, parade before you as their contemporaries saw them, in full panoply, with all their wordly glory — also, sometimes, less impressive aspects — captured on the canvas or in the stone. It is one of the best ways to get to know the people of another time; your walks through streets and lanes rich in history will be enlivened if you are able to visualize the men and women who made that history, whose actions and speech in the places you will visit helped to shape the world of the past and of the present — for this the collection also includes people of the early and middle twentieth century.

Kensington Palace
to Portobello Road

For Ease and for Dispatch, the Morning's best;
No Tides of Passengers the Street molest . . .
Now Industry awakes her busy Sons,
Full charg'd with News the breathless Hawker runs:
Shops open, Coaches roll, Carts shake the Ground,
And all the streets with passing Cries resound.

John Gay

AS THE epigraph suggests, this is a good walk to take in the early morning, especially if you can find a bright, sunny early spring or summer morning, because the first part takes you through London's largest green area, Hyde Park and Kensington Gardens. Later we'll get a sense of 'Industry' awakening, with hawkers, shops and carts aplenty.

You may begin this time from almost any entrance to the park or gardens, perhaps depending on which is closest to where you're staying, perhaps depending on how much walking you want to do, for if you start from Marble Arch or Hyde Park Corner you will be adding about a half a mile to the distance. Still, it will be through pleasant and peaceful districts, with traffic noise and smoke only in the distance; if you keep your eyes down on the grass and flowers and thus avoid the press of high-rise hotels that have grown up around the park like weeds, you will be able to imagine yourself in the country.

Much of Hyde Park belonged to the monks of Westminster Abbey until Henry VIII made it into a royal hunting park. The whole area has had an interesting history: sometimes it has been dangerous because of thieves who lurked upon the paths; it became a favourite duelling spot in the eighteenth century; and until the middle of the nineteenth century there were deer living in the park. Once a popular place for the gentry to ride and walk, to see and be seen, it has now become a popular gathering place for Londoners of every age and class, who may often feel, like Wordsworth, that they have been 'too long in city pent'. Despite its size, on a sunny Sunday it will be full of people, playing games, jogging, flying kites, feeding the birds, or just lying on the grass to soak up the sun. It is a marvellous place to retreat to when asphalt and concrete begin to get you down.

Together with Kensington Gardens, Hyde Park forms a continuous green space of over six hundred acres. Most London maps will show you the maze of pedestrian paths which criss-cross the area; in addition, there is no reason for you not to set off across country. Our first goal is the Albert Memorial, on the southern edge of Kensington Gardens. How you get there will depend on where you begin and your own inclinations.

If you enter the park at Marble Arch you will have the longest walk, perhaps a mile to the Albert Memorial. Still, it will be one of the most interesting. You begin at Speakers' Corner, the area where orators hold forth every day but especially on Sundays, on subjects ranging from the profound to the ridiculous. Traditionally, hecklers interrupt regularly, but there is seldom any physical violence; usually there are one or two police officers keeping a tolerant eye on things.

At this corner, too, you are near to 'Tyburn Tree', the permanent gallows that stood in this area for nearly six hundred years. Criminals in their carts rolled down Holborn and what is now Oxford Street from the Old Bailey prison and throngs of people waited here in a festive mood to enjoy the hanging. Such events took place here up until 1783; there is a plaque on the traffic island in the middle of the intersection to mark the spot.

But back to the more cheerful present. The first goal of this walk lies south-west from Marble Arch; you can choose which path you please or no path at all. The important thing to remember is that your way is blocked by the largest lake in the park and you must cross at the only bridge, in the middle, or else go a long way around.

As you cross the bridge, the Long Water will be on your right, the Serpentine on your left. There is a swimming beach, the Lido, on the south bank of the Serpentine, and boats can be rented for rowing or paddling. You will also find a restaurant just after you cross the bridge, as well as another at the eastern end of the Serpentine.

Once you cross the bridge, you are nearly at the Albert Memorial. Walk south until you hit Flower Walk, then turn west to the memorial.

If you have entered the park at Hyde Park Corner, at the south-east end, you will have a different and somewhat shorter walk to this point. You will first pass Apsley House (covered in more detail in Walk No. 4) and then move west along the edge of the park, with whatever detours to the north your energy or interest will sustain. The broad sandy road paralleling the westward course is Rotten Row, the famous equestrian path; you will notice mounting blocks at various places and you may also see a number of riders.

But a pleasant detour on your way to the Albert Memorial would be to head north-west to the Serpentine and to walk either along the north or south edge until you get to the bridge, after which, of course, you may proceed to the memorial, as described above.

Finally, if you entered the park from either the north-west corner of Notting Hill or the south-west corner of Kensington, you can proceed fairly directly to the Albert Memorial, leaving your exploration of this lovely green area to another day.

Albert was Queen Victoria's husband. Unlike some of the earlier kings and queens you may have read about, these two were genuinely in love and Victoria was inconsolable when Albert died in 1861, many years before her death.

Besides being a faithful adviser to his queen, Albert was a

ALBERT MEMORIAL

supporter of the arts; he is therefore memorialized not only here, but in the concert hall that bears his name across the road and the Victoria and Albert Museum beyond. The Victorians loved allegory, so you might like to examine the carvings around the statue. Various artists and men of letters are represented, and at the corners are groups representing Agriculture, Manufactures, Commerce and Engineering. At the foot of the steps appear groups of figures representing the world — the continents of Europe, Asia, Africa and America. You might find it interesting to try to decipher the meaning of these groups in more detail.

You might also wish to make your own aesthetic judgement about the memorial, which was erected on Queen Victoria's orders in 1872. Many critics have deplored the monument, considering it the worst kind of overblown Victoriana; others have admired its eclectic enthusiasm.

The area around the memorial is beautifully maintained and fortunately there seems to be no rule about not walking on the grass. You may like to sit and rest; if it's a sunny day, the park should be full of people enjoying the weather. If it's not a sunny day, you probably should be taking another walk.

At any rate, we will eventually leave Albert and walk the few steps to the delightful Floral Walk. Turn left, admiring the colourful display, and continue to the Broad Walk, which cuts north to your right.

The Broad Walk takes you straight to the eastern entrance of Kensington Palace, on the left, with the Round Pond to your right. This palace, and these gardens, are products of the eighteenth century. The palace itself was purchased by William III in 1689, just after he and Mary assumed the throne following the 'Glorious' or 'Bloodless' revolution that deposed James II, the Roman Catholic brother of Charles II. William moved here because he had an asthmatic condition and could not stand the smog in Westminster. From that time on, until the death of George II in 1760, Kensington Palace was the principal London residence of the reigning sovereign.

King William engaged Christopher Wren to make substantial changes to the property he had purchased from the Earl of Nottingham, and William Kent made further changes, both inside and out, in the early eighteenth century. Most of the exterior remains pretty much as Wren left it; a large part of the interior was redesigned by Kent, but there are lots of fine rooms designed by both men and some impressive decorations by the great wood carver, Grinling Gibbons.

Perhaps before you enter the palace grounds from the Long Walk, you should go round or at least look at the Round Pond. It is worth remembering that in the eighteenth century these were private gardens — people entered only by invitation. The gardens were originally laid out by George I, but Queen Caroline, the wife of George II, is chiefly responsible for the present arrangement. Today you are likely to find the Round Pond surrounded by children and their mothers — or nannies.

The gardens are beautiful and very well maintained. As you walk past the sunken garden up to the palace, you may feel a little like royalty yourself, especially as you watch the staff of gardeners working to keep it pruned and trimmed. But the palace itself is far more domestic, much more on a human scale, than most royal residences. It is hard, sometimes, to imagine how people really could have lived in some of those immense and draughty great halls, or held mundane conversations about the price of coffee in the midst of so much grandeur. But Kensington Palace is eminently liveable and, as you wander through looking at the mementoes of Queen Victoria, who was born here, you can almost envisage kings and queens sitting around discussing domestic affairs. But it may be more difficult to imagine getting to sleep in one of the state bedrooms, with their painted ceilings that would certainly encourage wakefulness if not nightmares.

Kensington Palace is still, of course, royal property and a royal residence. Princess Margaret lives here and so do the Prince and Princess of Wales, with their small children. It is in the private apartments that young William and Harry will begin to learn the privileged and responsible roles they will be expected to play in the world, as they also learn to play with their toys.

When you have finished your tour of Kensington Palace, you should leave to the west and you will soon find yourself in an area of 'Industry'. Here 'Shops open, Coaches roll, Carts shake the Ground'.

But Kensington Church Street, for most of its length, is a relatively quiet shopping area, chiefly known for its antiques. The shops are mostly small and a lot of them specialize in furnishings of a particular period, in silver or stamps, even in dolls. Others display a variety of antique merchandise. You can easily spend hours window shopping on your way north to Notting Hill Gate and you can enter any of the shops for a closer look if you wish, without fear that you would be pressurized into buying. In fact, some of the shopkeepers would be delighted just to show you their wares.

You will also find a number of small restaurants and pubs

along Kensington Church Street, particularly as you get near the top. If it is near lunch-time by now, this might be a very good place to stop.

Once you get to Notting Hill Gate, the busy road at the top, you will be close to our final destination in today's walk, the market in Portobello Road. You need to turn left at Notting Hill Gate, then first right keeping to the right on Pembridge Road as Kensington Park Road goes off to the left. Portobello Road will be the next turning on the left.

This has been the site of an open-air market, particularly for fruit and vegetables, for over a hundred years. On Saturday morning, the small antique dealers offer their wares on outdoor stalls. But you will find Portobello Road interesting any day of the week, for the stalls and for all the little shops that sell interesting and inexpensive souvenirs. It is always crowded, but on Saturday morning it becomes a solid mass of people; of course the people are part of the show. You may not find a first edition of Dickens at a bargain, but you will get a lot of inexpensive entertainment.

This is the end of the recommended walk, but of course you can continue if you are still full of energy. To the south and west runs Holland Walk, which leads past the remains of Holland House, the lovely wooded Holland Park and the Commonwealth Institute. Back the way we came is Kensington Gardens: there are always new places to explore there. But if you choose to finish here, the best place for public transport is Notting Hill Gate, which has an Underground station as well as a number of east–west buses and three or four that go north–south down Kensington Church Street. So it should be easy, with the help of your bus and Underground maps, to plot your route to your exact destination.

Nineteenth-Century
Prosperity

Dosn't thou 'ear my 'erse's legs, as they canters awaäy?
Proputty, proputty, proputty — that's what I'ears them saäy.

Tennyson

THIS WALK begins at Hyde Park Corner, one of London's
most traffic-jammed intersections, but will move very
quickly into a quieter and more dignified residential and
shopping area. Hyde Park Corner is easy to reach — there is
an Underground station and at least a dozen different buses
go there — but hard to get across. Fortunately, there is a
network of pedestrian subways to assist you. If you value
life and limb, use them.

Before leaving Hyde Park Corner you should note some
of the monuments in the area, a surprising number devoted
to the great 'Iron Duke' of Wellington, hero of Waterloo.
The triumphal Wellington Arch stands in the green space in
the centre of all these roads. An equestrian statue of the
duke also in this centre space faces Apsley House across the
road, on the corner of Hyde Park.

Apsley House was the London residence of the Duke of
Wellington; it has now become the Wellington Museum. It
was designed by Robert Adam in 1771 and purchased by the
duke in 1817. It is worth at least a brief visit to see the

APSLEY HOUSE

mementoes of his campaigns, including many valuable paintings and some incredibly beautiful china and silver services that were presented to him by the leaders of various European countries. And you can't miss the twice-lifesize naked statue of Napoleon, by the French sculptor Canova, with its fig-leaf that was added when the statue was brought to England.

Now, however, it is time to leave this busy intersection and plunge into the quiet splendour of Belgravia, a monument to the wealthy merchants of the nineteenth century who helped make commerce respectable. They built their mansions in this reclaimed area, the last part of central London to be drained and built on, next door to members of the peerage and newly elected Members of Parliament, who found Belgravia reasonably close to business.

We'll first walk south down Grosvenor Place, then turn first right at Grosvenor Crescent. We are now in Belgravia, a fashionable residential area in the mid-nineteenth century

45

BELGRAVE SQUARE

and still fashionable today, although many of the great mansions have either been taken over by embassies or offices, or broken up into small flats. Even today the peaceful quiet of this area and the impressive appearance of these town houses seem to come from another century. The loud traffic seems far away in both space and time.

As you walk around Wilton Crescent on your way south to the park-like area of Belgrave Square, it should be apparent that this is a planned community, with broad avenues, large expanses of greenery, all laid out in a geometrical grid, with wide access roads to the rest of the world.

Pause to look briefly up Belgrave Mews, to see one of the narrower streets, some of them still cobbled, that were erected at the back of the mansions as carriage yards, stables and servants' quarters. No one can afford such affluence now, so the former stables have been transformed into smaller flats for upwardly mobile families. They are still expensive, but offer a relatively affordable fashionable Belgravia address.

Belgrave Square comprises ten acres of grass and trees. As you continue south along either Belgrave Place or Upper Belgrave Street, you will soon cross Eaton Place, which television fans of 'Upstairs, Downstairs' will remember as the location of the Bellamy mansion.

The great houses, however, remain silent witnesses to a life-style that is long past. You might walk along Eaton Place, or the next street down, Eaton Square, and try to imagine how it must have been a hundred years ago when these houses sheltered the men and women whose beliefs and opinions did much to shape the pattern of English life.

Eaton Square is not a square at all; but the narrow gardens encompass more acres than Belgrave Square and their very tranquillity and stateliness help to define the qualify of the life that the former owners must have lived. The less fortunate London poor were tucked away in a distant part of the city, in the carriage houses behind these mansions — or downstairs in the servants' quarters.

As we have said, many of the owners of these houses were merchants, who had made their money in 'trade'. We'll move on now to some of the establishments which represent that kind of 'carriage trade' by walking south-west from Eaton Square across Cliveden Place to Sloane Square.

Sloane Square lacks the peace and quiet of Belgravia, for it is surrounded by shops, businesses, pubs and a famous old theatre, the Royal Court. It is also the boundary of Chelsea, which is the focus of Walk No. 18, that starts here. You may like to explore the square at this point, or else stop somewhere for a bit of rest and refreshment.

When you're ready to proceed once more, we'll head back, almost directly north, up Sloane Street. We're back in Belgravia here, but in the shopping area. This is where people who live in Belgravia buy their goods. If you like window shopping, you will enjoy walking up the west side of Sloane Street, admiring the items for sale and trying to ignore the price tags, which of course are rarely shown — if you need to ask the price you probably can't afford to buy the goods.

If you get tired of looking at the shops cross to the other side of the gardens on your right to Cadogan Place, where you will once more be in a quiet residential neighbourhood, with unhurried pedestrians walking dogs, and nannies

47

pushing prams. Unfortunately, you cannot walk in the gardens, because they belong to the residents who live along its edge, who get a key to the park with their deeds to their house.

Be sure, however, to return to Sloane Street before you reach Hans Crescent, which turns left just before Knightsbridge, through a few more fine old residential buildings. At its end, in Brompton Road, Hans Crescent will lead you to one of the chief goals of this walk, Harrods department store.

Harrods is more than a department store; it is an institution almost as venerable as the monarchy. Generations of wealthy and aristocratic people who have lived in Belgravia have shopped at Harrods. Belgravia has changed, of course, and so has Harrods, but you will still see the chauffeur-driven Rolls-Royces and Daimlers of the very rich waiting outside. But Harrods still has something for everyone: you can have your hair done, purchase theatre tickets, buy a comic greeting card or a genuine eighteenth-century print, order a layette or a funeral, spend a little or a lot.

Harrods is always worth a visit, whether you intend to buy or not, for in addition to being a symbol of the best in British merchandising, it is a genuine entertainment centre. You will certainly be impressed with the Scotch salmon, the plovers' eggs, the whole smoked turkeys, the cheeses and the charcuterie from around the world to be found in the Food Hall. In the clothing departments, you will find everything from the most outrageously avant-garde to the most rigidly conservative. And in the games department you may find just that special deck of cards or Parchesi set for a friend back home.

It is necessary, though, to pace yourself as carefully as if you were going round the British Museum. In the summer, there are dozens of tourists who simply squat on the floor near the exits, too exhausted from their shopping excursions to stand up. If you feel the need to sit, there are a number of good restaurants and snack bars; there is even a pub in the store. And of course there are other fine pubs nearby.

After you've finished with Harrods, if you still have enough energy to continue the walk — or are not too loaded down with packages — we will cross Brompton Road to reach another quiet residential district for the final part of this walk. But if you are interested in doing more shopping, it might be worth your while to go down Brompton Road for a short distance to Beauchamp Place, one of the most interesting little shopping streets in London.

Here you'll find a charming collection of small shops. There are china and jewellery shops, a number of lingerie and clothes shops, a fascinating place that specializes in old maps (with some less expensive reproductions as well), and a number of small restaurants and tea shops. Beauchamp Place is a short street; you can walk down one side and back up the other.

But to turn our back on the material pleasures of shopping, we will cross Brompton Road almost at Harrods' western corner, to Montpelier Street, and head north. Turn left at Montpelier Place and walk the short distance to its end. Then go left into Montpelier Walk and almost immediately right into Rutland Street. A few yards ahead on your right is the hole in the wall, a pedestrian passage that is the only way into Ennismore Gardens Mews and the residential area beyond. In the morning and evening this narrow opening is very busy with walkers hurrying to or from work.

The hole in the wall immediately transports you once more from busy Brompton Road into another quiet residential oasis. The streets are very narrow here, for the area is bounded on the north by even busier Knightsbridge. But here, too, there are pleasant gardens, charming little houses and the occasional quiet pub. Life seems to be run by a village clock, rather than at the hectic pace of one of the world's largest cities.

This secluded area seems a good place to end this walk, in another of the residential enclaves that London provides, whether by luck or good planning, in the midst of so many frantic commercial areas. This one is not quite as up-market as Belgravia, but it is friendly and hospitable; it is perhaps one of the few places in the city from which people walk to work. When it is time for you to return, you will find public transport close by. There are buses to be picked up on Kensington Road and Knightsbridge to the north, and Cromwell Road or Brompton Road to the south. There is an Underground station at the intersection of Knightsbridge and Sloane Street and another, South Kensington, just south of the Natural History Museum. This is just one of a group of fascinating museums, comprising the Victoria and Albert, Natural History, Science and Geological. But those deserve another day to themselves.

O bear me to the Paths of fair Pell-mell,
Safe are thy Pavements, grateful is thy Smell!
At distance, rolls along the gilded Coach,
Nor sturdy Carmen on thy Walks encroach;
No Lets should bar thy Ways, where Chairs deny'd
The soft Supports of Laziness and Pride;
Shops breathe Perfumes, thro' Sashes Ribbons glow,
The mutual Arms of Ladies, and the Beau.

John Gay

THIS WALK will begin at Piccadilly Circus and proceed through some of the most ancient and venerable royal monuments in London, ending finally at Parliament Square and Westminster Abbey. It does not cover many miles, but it includes a lot of history. Westminster Abbey and the Houses of Parliament should be saved for another time, for they deserve a full day of their own.

Getting to Piccadilly Circus should be easy by now. The walk begins westward, down the street called Piccadilly. A couple of shops are worth noting and perhaps visiting: Hatchard's bookshop at No. 187 is old and famous, and a reminder that this area, several hundred years ago, used to be a centre of bookselling. A little further along the same side of the street is Fortnum and Mason, the luxurious grocery store where the clerks wear frock coats; it was founded in 1770.

Still further west, across the street, the monumental building with a huge courtyard is Burlington House, built in 1665 by the Third Earl of Burlington, who was also

51

responsible for Chiswick House (see Walk No. 19), and who was the good friend of Alexander Pope, John Gay, Dr Arbuthnot and other members of that exclusive literary circle in the early eighteenth century. The house is now the home of the Royal Academy of Arts, which has a special exhibition of works by English painters every summer.

Next we need to backtrack a few steps and cross to the south side of Piccadilly once more, to visit St James's church, one of Christopher Wren's finest and the architect's own favourite of all his London churches. St James's was almost completely destroyed in the blitz of 1941, but many of its priceless artefacts, such as the Grinling Gibbons carved altarpiece and the organ, were hidden away and thus saved from destruction, and the church was restored after the war.

St James's was one of London's most fashionable churches in the eighteenth century; it is still fashionable and very popular with tourists today. William Blake was baptized here, in the marble font carved by Gibbons, and the organ came from Whitehall Palace, a gift of Queen

Mary in 1691 — two great musicians, John Blow and Henry Purcell, supervised its installation. It is likely that Handel played the organ, since he lived for eight years across the street in Burlington House. Sadly, the organ is not now playable, but your contribution in the offering box may go towards its repair.

St James's also has facilities for brass rubbing (entrance from the small street off Piccadilly behind the rectory) and there is a pleasant café called the Wren behind the church. In summer time there are tables in the churchyard where you may relax in relative quiet, close as you are to Piccadilly Circus.

After visiting the church, leave by the south side, either through the church or the café, and you will find yourself in Jermyn Street, one of the earliest streets laid out in this neighbourhood. It has a number of interesting small shops, some of which date back for several hundred years. Look for Paxton and Whitfield at No. 93, the cheese shop, Floris the perfumer, several shops that sell made-to-order shirts and a fine old-fashioned chemist. The cheese shop is worth a visit, for a glimpse — and smell — of the huge rounds of English Stilton and dozens of other fine cheeses from all over the world.

After window shopping, walk back to Duke of York Street (opposite St James's). If it is pub opening hours, you may like to pay a visit to the Red Lion, which has some of the finest Victorian engraved mirrors in London. It's a tiny place, but cheerful and usually crowded at lunch-time, with patrons spilling out over the pavement on sunny days.

As you continue down Duke of York Street, past the Red Lion, you will find yourself in St James's Square, a very fashionable place to live in the eighteenth century. Most of the houses here are original, although many of them have been altered in a variety of ways and most of them have become offices or clubs. The Libyan Embassy was in this square (in the corner to your right as you enter from Duke of York Street); this was the scene of the shooting and siege in 1984. You will be able to discover many interesting historical facts about the square by walking around and reading the blue plaques. General Eisenhower had his headquarters here for a time during the last war, for example. As you pass Charles II Street on the east side of the square, look up towards Haymarket for a fine view of the Haymarket Theatre.

This whole area that we are now exploring is known as St James's. It was laid out in more or less its present shape, chiefly as a residential area adjacent to the palace of St James, by the Earl of St Albans in 1670. His family name was Jermyn — hence the name of the shopping street we have just left. In the late seventeenth century, the area was particularly fashionable for bachelors' lodgings; it remained primarily residential until the nineteenth century, when many of the expensive houses were turned into gentlemen's clubs. We'll see some of those clubs as we move south now to Pall Mall.

Both Pall Mall, the principal thoroughfare of St James's, and the Mall, just south, which leads to Buckingham Palace, take their name from a game that was played in the time of Henry VIII — a kind of cross between croquet and golf. As you enter Pall Mall from St James's Square, you may wish to turn left up to Waterloo Place, where you can look south to the Duke of York's Column. It was built in the early nineteenth century to honour 'the soldier's friend', the second son of George III and Commander-in-Chief of the British Army from 1795–1827; every soldier in the army contributed one day's pay to cover the cost of the monument. At this point you have a fine view towards Westminster, across Carlton House Terrace, one of the most exclusive residential areas in London, as well as a corner of St James's Park, where we'll be walking in a few moments.

After admiring the view, turn back to Pall Mall and make your way down to its end, to St James's Palace. Along the way you will pass many imposing buildings, residences in the eighteenth century, mostly private clubs now. These are mostly so exclusive (and usually still 'men only') that they don't even put their names out front, but on the south side, as you walk from Waterloo Place, you will pass the Athenaeum, the Traveller's, the Reform, the Royal Automobile, and the Oxford and Cambridge. Across the

BURLINGTON HOUSE

street are the Junior Carlton Club (for people on the waiting list for the Carlton Club) and the Army and Navy Club. Perhaps more interesting, the painter Gainsborough lived at No. 80 from 1774 until his death, and No. 79 was given to Nell Gwynn by Charles II — so they could talk over the fence from her garden to his. There's a painting of such a scene in the Victoria and Albert Museum, together with a disapproving quote from the diarist, John Evelyn, who presumably watched the scene.

St James's Palace, at the end of Pall Mall, is not open to the public, but you may walk through the courtyards as you make your way south to the Mall. There has been a palace here since 1531, when Henry VIII first built here; the site had previously been a hospital for young women with leprosy. Christopher Wren did some major remodelling, and the palace became the official London residence of the sovereign in 1698, when the palace at Whitehall burned down; the American ambassador to Great Britain is still designated 'Ambassador to the Court of St James. The palace is now used for various court functions, including the proclamation of a new monarch from a balcony in Friary Court, and it is the residence of certain members of the court. It is guarded by the same regiment which patrols

Buckingham Palace, but without quite as much ceremony when the guards are changed.

After St James's Palace, make your way south to the Mall via Marlborough Road. The large building on the left is Marlborough House, built by Christopher Wren for the famous Duke of Marlborough in 1709. On the right is Clarence House, built by Nash in 1825; it is the residence of the queen mother.

Now we're in the stately Mall, a broad avenue lined with a double row of plane trees that leads from Admiralty Arch at Charing Cross to Buckingham Palace, the present London home of Queen Elizabeth II. The Queen rides up the Mall for her birthday celebration in June; the wedding procession of Prince Charles and Princess Diana moved up the Mall on its way to St Paul's Cathedral. And occasionally you can see horse-drawn carriages rolling up the Mall to bring foreign dignitaries to an audience with the Queen.

At this point, if you wish, you may follow the broad avenue up to Buckingham Palace; perhaps, if it is nearly noon, you will be in time for the changing of the guard, which begins at 11.30. You may even want to stop at this point and pick up the rest of the walk another day. If so, you will find many buses and an Underground station to your left at Charing Cross, or, if you go right up to the palace, you may continue south around the left side of the palace for about a quarter of a mile to Victoria Station, which also provides lots of public transport.

To continue, however, or pick up at this point, retrace your steps down the Mall until you are opposite Marlborough Road and enter St James's Park on your right. (If you did not visit Buckingham Palace, you can simply cross the street when you emerge from St James's Palace.) Take the road straight ahead, south, and in a short distance you will find yourself at the lake that runs through the centre of the park, a haven for wildfowl of all kinds.

St James's Park was laid out in the early sixteenth century by Henry VIII, in an area extending from his old palace in Whitehall to his newly built palace at St James's. It was, of course, surrounded by elegant residences occupied by his

HORSE GUARDS

friends — and mistresses. It has been the site of many historical moments: Charles I walked across the park from St James's Palace to his execution in Whitehall in 1649; his son, Charles II, enjoyed walking there after his restoration to the throne in 1660 — Pepys saw his new sovereign there for the first time in that year and noted the occasion in his diary. Charles II opened the park to the public and ever since it has been a favourite place for a pleasant midday stroll. If you want to sit down for a rest, bear in mind that a chair may cost you a hire charge — the custom dates back to 1785.

Having rested your feet, cross the little lake, or 'canal', by the suspension bridge, pausing briefly in the middle to enjoy the view. With your back towards Buckingham Palace, straight ahead you can see the pearl-grey stone buildings of the Horse Guards Parade, with some of Whitehall behind; slightly to the right you can see the more monumental architecture of the Foreign Office, with the tower of Big Ben and Westminster Abbey in the distance. As much as anywhere, this is the centre of royal London.

Continue straight ahead after crossing the bridge. You will soon find yourself out of the park, on Birdcage Walk, which runs along the south boundary and is named after the royal aviary that was kept here by James I. Cross Birdcage Walk and continue south; you will find yourself almost at once in Queen Anne's Gate, a small street to the left that contains some of the finest eighteenth-century houses still standing in London. Walk along this street and you will get a good sense of the domestic architecture of this period; you can see some of the old torch holders over the doors and metal torch extinguishers. On the right is a statue of Queen Anne herself, which has been here since the first decade of the eighteenth century when she was still alive.

At the end of this short block, turn left again up the narrow Cockpit Steps and you will be back in Birdcage Walk. Westminster Square is just to your right now; you could walk there directly down Great George Street. But this walk will take one more detour before it reaches that destination.

Turn left just a little, then, down Birdcage Walk, until you find another entrance to the park. We will now be cutting across the south-east corner until we come out on Horse Guards Road. Downing Street, the residence of the prime minister, runs east at this point, but it is usually blocked off by the police. You can see the door of Number 10, however, from the other side, from Parliament Street.

Our route will take us a little further up Horse Guards Road to the Horse Guards Parade, where the Queen reviews her troops on her official birthday in June. The buildings beyond the parade, which date back to the eighteenth century, are the barracks where the monarch's household guards live; they depart here for the changing of the guard at Buckingham Palace every morning at eleven. There are also both foot and mounted guards in front, replaced every hour and every second hour. You may walk from Horse Guards Road straight up through the parade (used as a car park most days), and on through the main archway out into Whitehall.

Directly across the street when you emerge from the Horse Guards building is the Banqueting House, the last surviving remnant of the old Whitehall Palace, the rest of which burned to the ground in 1798. Since the name 'White Hall' means a place of entertainment, it is appropriate that only the Banqueting House survives. It has the distinction of being the first building in London that was designed in the classic tradition of Italy. The architect was Inigo Jones, who built it in the early years of the seventeenth century; the style came to be called Palladian after the Italian architect Andrea Palladio. This was the style that was to dominate English public architecture in the following century.

The Banqueting House is open to the public. Inside, you will probably be most interested in the magnificent painted ceiling that was created for Charles I by Rubens. Ironically enough, allegories are depicted which celebrate the glorious reigns of James I and his son Charles I. In fact it was from a window in this same Banqueting Hall that Charles I stepped to his death on the scaffold that was built in the street outside.

Returning outside, we can look down Whitehall towards Parliament Square and get a sense of the importance of this thoroughfare in British history. It has always been a principal route from the City to Westminster and, since Henry VIII moved his court here in the mid-sixteenth century, it has been a centre of government — the monumental buildings on both sides of the street testify to this. On the right, below Horse Guards, are the Treasury, the Foreign Office and the Home Office, where Churchill had his War Room, which is now open to the public; on the left are newer office buildings, built to accommodate the overflow of civil servants from across the street.

About halfway down, in the middle of the street, stands the Cenotaph, a monument commemorating the men and women who gave their lives in the two world wars of this century. At about this point Whitehall becomes Parliament Street, which very soon opens out to Parliament Square.

Parliament Square is the end of this walk, although the beginning of much more exploration another time. It is unlikely that anyone would feel like investigating any of these great public buildings right now. Meanwhile, to return to your starting point should be easy. There are dozens of buses that pass this point and there is an Underground station, Westminster, just around the corner to the left, before the bridge.

Parliament Square
to the Tate Gallery

> Yet let me not descend to trivial Song,
> Nor vulgar Circumstance my Verse prolong;
> Why should I teach the Maid when Torrents pour,
> Her Head to shelter from the sudden Show'r?

John Gay

WHY SHOULD it be necessary to tell you when to come in out of the rain? But since this walk is largely concerned with the Tate Gallery, and most of your time will be spent indoors, it is a good one to consider if the skies look grey, or if you are expecting a sudden shower. On days like this, don't forget to take along those other tools of the walker's trade — an efficient umbrella and perhaps a folded-up plastic raincoat. These emergency raincoats weigh only a few ounces and take up only a few inches of space in a bag or a pocket.

This walk begins at Parliament Square — assuming that the rains have not yet descended and that a short stroll in the fresh air seems desirable. It should be noted that the half mile given as the distance describes only the length of the walk from Parliament Square to the Tate; the amount of walking you do in the Tate itself will be up to you.

We begin at Parliament Square simply because it is such a marvellous place to begin. You will find your steps returning to this historic area often — when you visit Westminster Abbey, or when you queue up to listen to a debate in the House of Commons, when you are planning a trip on the river, or when you simply wish to contemplate the Thames from the excellent vantage point of Westminster Bridge.

This is a lovely area, well deserving of many visits. You'll find something new each time. Perhaps the light will be different, or you'll come upon it from a different angle, and a different beauty will appear to your eyes. But should the weather demand you start with the Tate, and the skies clear up later, consider reversing the walk and ending up at Parliament Square.

When you leave the square, go south down St Margaret Street, with the Houses of Parliament and the river on your left. The very old parish church of St Margaret's will be on your right, dating from the fifteenth century, the official church of the House of Commons; it has always been a popular place to get married. Samuel Pepys was married here, as were John Milton and Winston Churchill. Inside there are many monuments, including one to Sir Walter Raleigh. And there is a splendid Dutch stained glass window, very old, depicting the bethrothal of Catherine of Aragon to Prince Arthur, the eldest son of Henry VII.

Across the street from St Margaret's, in a narrow garden behind Westminster Hall, is a statue of Oliver Cromwell, Lord Protector of the Commonwealth during the years of the interregnum, 1653–8, the only time in modern history that Britain has been without an hereditary monarch. Since you have already seen the statue of Charles I at Charing Cross, you should take a look at the man who was largely responsible for his beheading.

As you continue south, St Margaret's Street broadens out into Old Palace Yard on your left, a reminder again that this area was once not a parliament but an ancient palace. Across the street is another reminder, the squat Jewel Tower, one of the few survivals from the medieval Palace of Westminster, dating from the fourteenth century. Originally a storehouse for royal treasures, this tower was later used by government in a variety of ways. It is not used now, but it has some interesting old stonework inside, as well as artefacts from the surrounding area.

At the south end of Old Palace Yard, as you enter Abingdon Street, the Victoria Tower Gardens will be on your left, a pleasant place to pause if the weather is good. It offers excellent views of the Thames and two bridges — Westminster down river and Lambeth up river.

About halfway along Victoria Gardens, take Great Peter Street to the right. There are some fine Georgian houses along this street and, if you turn left down Lord North Street, you will soon find yourself in Smith Square, dominated by the unusual eighteenth-century church of St John the Evangelist. It has a strange shape for a parish church — hard to see now because of the surrounding buildings — a square with a tower at each corner. Not everyone likes it; Dickens called it 'a petrified monster on its back with its legs in the air'. But it is an interesting architectural oddity, now used for lectures and concerts.

If you go east of Smith Square down Dean Stanley Street, you will get the most unobstructed view of the church and you will soon find yourself back at the river, at Millbank. This is the shortest route to the Tate; if you turn right you will be there in about a quarter of a mile, past Lambeth Bridge and the all-glass Millbank Tower (at 387 feet, one of the tallest buildings in London) and past Queen Alexandra Hospital.

But Millbank, for all its pleasant views of the river, can be noisy and full of traffic. If you prefer a quieter walk to the Tate, turn south out of Smith Square down Dean Bradley Street and then right down Horseferry Road, which leads to Lambeth Bridge and reminds us that before the bridge was built there was a substantial ferry here for horses and wagons.

Keep walking until Horseferry Road makes a sharp turn to the right, then take either Rutherford Street or Maunsell Street to the left; they both lead to the very large Vincent Square, used now as a playground for Westminster School. To your right, along the north side of the square, are the buildings of the Royal Horticultural Society, which has flower shows at various times during the year.

To get to the Tate Gallery from here, leave the square by Vincent Street to the east, turn right down Marsham Street and left at Bulinga Street, which runs alongside the Tate. The entrance is from Millbank.

The Tate Gallery houses the national collection of British painting, arranged generally in a chronological order, as well as a fine collection of modern painting, both British and continental, from the Impressionists to the present. Like all great art galleries, it is impossible to take in everything in one day. It is best to choose a period or a painter to concentrate on and plan to come back another time.

On this principle of selectivity, we'll mention only a few special items out of England's golden age of painting, the eighteenth century. There are representative examples from all the great painters of this period — Hogarth, Allan Ramsay, Gainsborough, Sir Joshua Reynolds (first president of the Royal Academy), Richard Wilson, Stubbs

SIR JOSHUA REYNOLDS

(the remarkable painter of animals), Wright of Derby and Romney. The collection of paintings by J.M.W. Turner is the most comprehensive in existence. It is almost a museum in itself, a history of painting styles from the late eighteenth to the early nineteenth centuries, as Turner moved from conventional portraiture and landscapes to impressionism.

Several of William Hogarth's most famous paintings are here, including the famous *Self-portrait with Pug* and *The Graham Children*, the latter seemingly a simple family portrait until the viewer begins to comprehend the significance of the peripheral parts of the painting, which cast a sombre pall over the depiction of happy childhood. You remember that this is the man who produced the powerful *Gin Lane* and *Harlot's Progress*.

When you look at the portraits of Reynolds, Gainsborough, Ramsay and Highmore, you will get a glimpse of the domestic life of another age; you will see not only kings and queens, dukes and duchesses but middle-class businessmen and their families, men who were developing England's commerce and whose confidence in their social position now enabled them to adopt the traditions of family portraiture that had formerly been the province of the aristocracy.

Such paintings by Stubbs as *Mares and Foals in a Landscape* are further evidence of the democratization of art, and Wright of Derby's famous representation of *Experiment with the Air-Pump* shows the eighteenth-century fascination with science. And the charming, often breathtaking, landscapes that were a favourite subject show yet again how painting in this period could exalt everyday subjects. You may wish to look particularly closely at some of Constable's paintings of Hampstead, since Walk No. 17 will take you there; some of the views seem to have changed very little in the last two hundred years.

These recommendations are offered merely as one possibility. If you would prefer on this first visit to look at some of the earlier paintings or at some of the more recent works, that should be your choice. And the Tate always has special exhibitions that are worth the small admission charge. But wherever you go in the Tate, as in all great galleries, you will experience a great sense of original discovery when you stand in front of a painting that you have seen in reproduction for many years. That's what makes visiting galleries so rewarding.

When pictures finally tire you, the Tate has an excellent, although rather expensive restaurant, as well as an inexpensive café. It also has a fine shop with colour slides and printed reproductions of many of the gallery's pictures, as well as a variety of splendid art books.

Public transport from the Tate is not too good, although a short walk north up Vauxhall Bridge Road will take you to Victoria, where there are buses, trains and the Underground. You can find the No. 88 bus outside the gallery on Millbank that will take you to Trafalgar Square or Piccadilly. Pimlico Underground station, on the Victoria line, is not far from the river, just off Vauxhall Bridge Road. If it is still raining, unfurl your umbrella; the taxis will be as scarce as an open pub at midnight.

Mayfair

Let others in the jolting Coach confide,
Or in the leaky Boat the Thames divide;
Or, box'd within the Chair, contemn the Street,
Still let me walk . . .

John Gay

OUR WALK today is through one of the most fashionable
residential areas of London, from the eighteenth century,
when its streets and squares were first laid out, until today.
Perhaps it is no accident that it borders to the north-west on
Speakers' Corner in Hyde Park, where orators often
fulminate against wealth and privilege; but surely their
voices do not reach those who live in Mayfair.

Sydney Smith, the economist, once asserted that the area
between Oxford Street to the north and Piccadilly to the
south, between Hyde Park to the west and Regent Street to
the east, 'enclosed more intelligence and ability, to say
nothing of wealth and beauty, than the world had ever
collected into such a space before'. This is Mayfair, the area
we will explore today, named for the May Fair that was held
here from very ancient times until the end of the eighteenth
century, when it became too rowdy for its neighbours and
was forbidden by George III.

We'll start at busy Hyde Park Corner, but we'll get away
from the noisy traffic straight away. Starting from the
north-east corner, walk a few steps up Piccadilly to Old Park
Lane, turn left and you will find yourself almost at once in
relative quiet.

But the respite is temporary, for you will soon find yourself on the southbound leg of busy Park Lane, the wide boulevard that stretches north between Hyde Park and Mayfair. Some of London's most luxurious hotels are on Park Lane; their best rooms have a view of the park. You have already passed the Hotel Intercontinental at Hyde Park Corner and slipped behind the Inn on the Park; the London Hilton will soon be on your right.

A little further along stands the imposing Dorchester, a marvellous place to have tea any afternoon, a truly Edwardian experience with little sandwiches and cakes served by frock-coated waiters while a piano tinkles in the background. Adjacent to the Dorchester is a bank that looks like a castle, a case of form not following function but location.

But Mayfair has much to offer besides the sight of oil-rich Arabs dismounting from Rolls-Royces and Bentleys in front of these expensive hotels. We'll leave Park Lane and turn east on Curzon Street, heading for the site of the old May Fair, an area of crooked narrow streets now called Shepherd Market, named not because shepherds once congregated here but after a man named Shepherd who used to run a market on the site.

Continue along Curzon Street, past an interesting mixture of modern office buildings and older, remodelled eighteenth- or nineteenth-century mansions, past Chesterfield Street on your left, until you find one of several narrow lanes that lead on the right to Shepherd Market. We're now in the central area of the old May Fair. Here the narrow lanes, small shops, pubs and restaurants give evidence of a world quite different from the wealth and luxury we have recently left.

Shepherd Market contains an interesting collection of small shops, selling everything from tourist souvenirs to fresh fish. Its character is almost downmarket compared to that of Mayfair as a whole. It seems like a small village dropped into the middle of a sophisticated city — it goes its own way at its own pace. The rather raffish quality of the streets might serve to remind you that this was (and is today) a red-light district of London — the ladies settled close to their well-heeled customers.

Several pubs are worth noting, including the Bunch of Grapes, which has benches outside in the summertime, and Shepherd's Tavern, with comfortable seats and a sedan chair converted to a telephone booth. If you wondered about the line in the epigraph at the beginning of this walk, 'box'd within the Chair', try making a telephone call in Shepherd's Tavern and you'll get a sense of how small the sedan chair conveyances were. This one is rather elegant; it is reputed to have been owned by one of George III's sons.

When you have seen enough of Shepherd Market, return the way you came to Curzon Street; turn north along Queen Street until you reach Charles Street. Turn right and you will find yourself in Berkeley Square. This has always been one of the most exclusive residential centres of Mayfair.

If you walk around the square you'll see a number of blue plaques identifying the famous people who have lived here. On the south-west corner, for example, where we entered the square, stands a house that belonged to the Earl of Shelburne, the prime minister who conceded the independence of the new United States. On the west side, Winston Churchill grew up in No. 48 and William Pitt, the great eighteenth-century prime minister, resided at No. 47.

If you went east from here you would move from residential to commercial Mayfair — here are all the fine and expensive shops that you might expect to find in such an elegant district. Bond Street runs from Piccadilly to Oxford Street; it is Old Bond Street for a short distance and then New Bond Street for the rest of its length.

Here and in the adjacent streets you will find everything your heart could desire and which your chequebook cannot afford. There are art galleries, selling genuine old masters as well as new works, jewellery shops, perfumeries, dress shops, Rolls-Royce showrooms, auction rooms. Everything is expensive, and probably worth it. A little further east, parallel to Bond Street, runs Savile Row, the name that is synonymous with fine tailoring for gentlemen. The tailors are still there, but — to the chagrin of some — they have now been joined by a few shops that sell suits off the peg. A sad come-down for the street.

We will leave the shopping to those who are enthusiastic about it, however, and continue north through the attractive residential area. If you leave Berkeley Square to the west, via Hill Street, turning right then left into Farm Street, you will soon come to one of the main north–south avenues, South Audley Street.

Turning right on South Audley Street will bring you almost at once in front of a small and unpretentious church, the Grosvenor Chapel. It is an old church with some claims to fame. It was the burial place of Lady Mary Wortley Montagu, the eighteenth-century woman of letters who introduced smallpox vaccination to England after her stay in Turkey, and of John Wilkes, the controversial eighteenth-century politician and self-styled 'friend of liberty'.

The United States armed forces used this church as their chapel during the Second World War because it was close to 'Little America', the site of the American Embassy in Grosvenor Square. The most pleasant way to get there is around the Grosvenor Chapel on the left to the peaceful Mount Street Gardens. At the east end of the gardens you can turn north via Carlos Place into Grosvenor Square.

The American Embassy is the massive building on the west side of the square, dominated by the huge sculpture of an eagle on top. Most of the large office buildings around the square are for embassy staff; for this reason the area is known as Little America. You can also find a splendid statue of America's wartime president, Franklin Delano Roosevelt, on the north side of the square.

Although most of these buildings are modern, you can still find a few attractive older structures nestling among the giants. On the north-east corner, for example, No. 9 was the residence of the American John Adams when he was ambassador to the Court of St James.

If you are feeling the need of sustenance by this time, you may backtrack down South Audley Street to Mount Street, where you will find the Audley, a splendid Victorian pub with a beautiful mahogany interior. It was renovated in the nineteenth century to the criteria set by the aristocratic leaseholder, who felt that only the most genteel and elegant

71

NEW CHURCH, NORTH AUDLEY STREET

décor would be suitable for this area.

At this point the walk is nearly over. Perhaps the best way to finish is to work your way east, by way of Mount Street if you have visited the Audley, or by way of Grosvenor Street if you haven't, to Davies Street, and turn left. You'll pass Claridges Hotel on your right, where all the diplomats stay, and very soon you'll be in Oxford Street, near the Bond Street Underground station, with access to dozens of buses.

Oxford Street, after Mayfair, is another world entirely. Unlike the shops of Mayfair, those on Oxford Street are crowded with people and bargains; here you will find commerce on a grand scale in its less attractive form.

A short distance west along Oxford Street is Selfridges department store, which has a façade nearly as impressive as Harrods. If Harrods is the temple of the rich, Selfridges is the church of the middle class. Upper middle class at that — there is nothing cheap about Selfridges. But on Oxford Street outside there are cut-price shops and street sellers, chain store outlets and souvenir stands. This is commerce at its most frantic; cool elegance has been left behind in Mayfair.

Legal London

Happy Augusta! Law-defended Town!
Here no dark Lanthorns shade the Villain's Frown;
Here Tyranny ne'er lifts her purple Hand,
But Liberty and Justice guard the Land;
No Bravos here profess the bloody Trade,
Nor is the Church the Murd'rer's Refuge made.

John Gay

THIS WALK will visit both the law courts of London, where
you may sit in on a trial if the courts are in session, and the
Inns of Court, formerly universities of the law, now offices
for barristers and solicitors. The former wear gowns and
wigs and plead in the courtrooms; the latter work behind the
scenes, preparing the material used by the barristers.
English law is steeped in tradition and history. Today we'll
look at some ancient places and customs.

The starting point is Holborn, where the Underground
station is served by both the Piccadilly and Central lines.
There are many buses as well, both those that go down
Oxford Street and continue to High Holborn and those that
come up Kingsway from the Strand in the south.

Once you get to the intersection of High Holborn and
Kingsway, you should walk south along Kingsway just a
short distance until you find a short, narrow street to the left
called Remnant Street. This will lead you to Lincoln's Inn
Fields, our first destination.

Lincoln's Inn Fields is a large green square that has been

here for centuries. Despite John Gay's assurance that 'No Bravos here profess the bloody Trade', it was a dangerous place to walk either by day or night in the eighteenth century. In another part of the poem, Gay advises walkers not to take a 'link boy', someone who walked ahead with a lighted torch, through Lincoln's Inn Fields, because he was probably in league with the footpads and would lead you into their clutches.

In the early days, Lincoln's Inn Fields was also a place of execution — the bloody kind, involving drawing and quartering. But it is a peaceful place today, where secretaries from the surrounding offices sunbathe at noon and barrister's assistants eat their lunch. It also has a number of interesting and historic buildings on its perimeter.

Walk straight ahead, down the west side of the square. No. 58, with its tall windows and pillars, was the home of John Forster, the friend and biographer of Charles Dickens; it was here that Dickens gave one of his first readings from his own works and thus embarked upon a new career as a reader.

This is Dickens country: if you continue out of the square along this side, shortly you will come to 'The Old Curiosity Shop', which has all kinds of Dickens memorabilia and souvenirs. It is not, of course, the shop that Dickens described in his novel, but it well represents a typical small nineteenth-century shop.

Chancery Lane, which runs just to the east of Lincoln's Inn Fields, is the location of many scenes in Dickens's dark novel, *Bleak House*, while the Courts of Chancery, which occupy the position of chief villain in that novel, were in Dickens's time in Lincoln's Inn, the Inn of Court that we will soon be visiting. The other literary association you might want to make with this area concerns John Mortimer's *Rumpole* stories published by Penguin Books and televised by the BBC. Rumpole, an ageing barrister, keeps chambers in one of the Inns of Court and pleads his cases in the Old Bailey, which we will visit at the end of this walk. John Mortimer, a barrister as well as a writer, has his chambers in the Middle Temple, which we will also visit.

There is much more to see and admire around Lincoln's Inn Fields. On the north side, No. 13 is the Soane Museum, one of London's most fascinating — and little known — museums. The house was designed as his own residence by Sir John Soane, an eminent architect of the eighteenth century, who was responsible for the Bank of England (now surrounded by an outer ring of buildings, so his design can no longer be seen from the street) and who planned a completely new design for the old Whitehall Palace, which was never built.

Among other things, Sir John Soane was an inveterate collector of ancient antiquities and anything else he could lay his hands on, and his house, in accordance with the terms of his will, eventually became a museum to show his collection. It has a double interest for the visitor: it is, on the ground floor and above, a well-furnished eighteenth-century house, which thus provides a glimpse of how a wealthy Englishman of that period lived. In addition, the lower basement floor is a museum showing a wide range of ancient treasures, as well as some from Soane's own time. When you visit the museum, make sure you see the paintings by Hogarth. Here is the complete collection of one of Hogarth's most important series, *The Rake's Progress*, as well as all four paintings in the series called *The Election*.

You may want to save the Soane Museum for another day, since this walk offers many other sights. When you leave Lincoln's Inn Fields, walk along the southern side, past the monumental buildings of the Royal College of Surgeons and go straight through the archway at the end into the first Inn of Court, called Lincoln's Inn.

The Inns of Court are no longer places of legal instruction, but they are still places where barristers and solicitors have their offices. To qualify as a barrister, the candidate normally must be affiliated with one of the Inns. Thus they are still important law centres and — as you will see once you pass through this gate into Lincoln's Inn — they still have something of the peaceful, ivy-covered quality of traditional universities.

On your left as you walk through the gate is the dining

hall, where many of the members dine and where the younger members must take a certain number of dinners to be introduced to the Inn. Beyond that is the library. Directly ahead of you as you enter is the Old Hall, where the Court of Chancery sat in Dickens's time; to its left is the chapel. If you wish, you may walk up to the left to admire the old buildings; the gardens directly ahead are open only at lunch-time.

The chapel is also open at lunch-time, but it was built in this century, for the old chapel was one of the few buildings in London bombed out in the First World War. The Old Hall was built in the late fifteenth century and is the oldest building in this complex. It now is divided into offices.

Continue south, through New Square, with its original gas lamps, and between the entrances numbered 3 and 4 you will find a narrow passage leading out of Lincoln's Inn. Both sides of the passageway house a legal bookshop; in addition to the law books in the window they usually have a display of cartoons, with barristers as the butt of the jokes. This might be a good place to pick up a gift for a lawyer friend.

When you emerge from the passage you will find yourself in Carey Street. If you wish, take a brief detour here to the left and then left again into Star Yard. A few steps up on the right side of the street is an interesting shop that sells formal wigs to barristers and judges. You might like to take a close look in the shop window at the small wig with pigtails worn by barristers — it is harder to examine them closely when they are worn by a man or a woman. The wearing of these wigs is a very old tradition, but it is still required today when appearing in a courtroom.

Coming back from Star Yard, turn right again along Carey Street and continue past the entrance to Lincoln's Inn for a little way. The old pub here called the Seven Stars is usually full of lawyers at noon and in the early evening; it has many fine old prints on the walls inside — of lawyers from the past and of characters from Dickens's novels. This might be a place for a brief stop, but there will be other pubs and restaurants when we reach Fleet Street.

The monumental building across the street from the Seven Stars is the Royal Courts of Justice, one of two

OLD TEMPLE BAR

principal buildings in London where trials are held. These are the civil courts, where litigation chiefly concerns property. The Central Criminal Court is in the Old Bailey, some half mile to the east, where this walk will end.

You may enter the law courts a short distance down Carey Street from the pub; if you want to sit in on a civil trial, you have only to walk into one of the many courtrooms. You are likely to find them rather boring, even though they are bread and butter for the lawyers involved.

When you have seen enough of the law courts, go out the other side, to Fleet Street; as you leave, turn round and look at the building. It is a very impressive neo-Gothic structure, with an exuberant display of towers and turrets and crenellations.

You're now at the beginning of Fleet Street, the extension of the Strand from Charing Cross. In the middle of the street where you emerge stands a monument with a griffin on top marking the separation between Westminster (to your right) and the City (to your left). This is Temple Bar. For centuries a real barrier stood here, the last one designed by Christopher Wren and removed — mainly to ease the flow of traffic — in 1880.

Temple Bar used to mark a real separation; the monarch would always stop here and ask permission of the Lord Mayor of London to continue. The custom is still ceremonially observed. The spikes on the top of Temple Bar used to display the heads of traitors, a grim warning to those of dubious loyalty.

But Fleet Street is very noisy, so we'll cross the road and head for the next Inns of Court, Inner and Middle Temples. There are two entrances: Middle Temple Lane and Inner Temple Lane. Middle Temple Lane is a little further right, or east; it can be identified by the carving above, all that is left of Wren's gatehouse — you can see the lamb that is the badge of the Middle Temple and the date, 1694.

To the west, above the entrance to Inner Temple Lane, is a fine example of an early seventeenth-century half-timbered house, one of the few such houses in the City to survive the disastrous fire of 1666. It is now called Prince Henry's Room, referring to the oldest son of James I, and it is open to visitors on weekday afternoons. There is a fine plaster ceiling and an exhibition of Pepys manuscripts; Samuel Pepys was born not far from here.

We continue our walk by proceeding down Middle Temple Lane and into Middle Temple, named after the original holders of the property in the Middle Ages, the Knights Templars, a religious and military order that took part in the Crusades. Continue down Middle Temple Lane for a short distance until you find a passageway to the right leading to Fountain Court. On your left is the hall of the Middle Temple, built in the late sixteenth century. In February 1602 Shakespeare himself may well have performed here in the première of his play, *Twelfth Night*. Beyond, at the fountain, we are in Dickens country again – he describes it in *Martin Chuzzlewit*.

Returning to Middle Temple Lane, we'll continue until the fine stretch of gardens appears on the left. These are Inner Temple Gardens, not open to the public, but as you walk along above them you can get a good view of the many roses which grow there in the summer and of the Thames.

When you get beyond Inner Temple Gardens, turn right into King's Bench Walk. Most of the buildings here were

TEMPLE CHURCH

put up soon after the Great Fire, in the late seventeenth or early eighteenth century; you can sometimes find dates in the stonework. These are now lawyers' chambers; you may find it interesting to read some of the names, perhaps to find out how many — or how few — are women.

After you have looked at King's Bench Walk, head back up towards Fleet Street. Near the top, walk through a short tunnel to your left and you will see Temple Church on your right. Temple Church is one of the few round churches in England, built in the twelfth century in the style of the Holy Sepulchre in Jerusalem. It was largely destroyed in the last war, but it has been handsomely restored. Inside, you can see stone effigies of medieval knights. Don't miss the extraordinary gargoyles around the walls.

When you leave the church, walk around the front and back along the other side to find two tombs, one very elaborate of a long-forgotten lawyer and one very simple, almost concealed, of the eighteenth-century poet and playwright, Oliver Goldsmith. Stone monuments clearly do not confer fame or immortality.

SAMUEL JOHNSON

After visiting the Goldsmith grave, return to Fleet Street via Inner Temple Lane, the one beneath Prince Henry's Room. On your left, just a short distance before you emerge into Fleet Street, you should be able to find an office with a name-plate identifying one of its tenants as John Mortimer, the creator of *Rumpole of the Bailey*.

In Fleet Street, turn right. We'll head now with only a couple of detours to our last destination, the Old Bailey.

If it is lunch-time, you might visit the famous old tavern, the Cheshire Cheese. It is just across the street and up a narrow alley at 145 Fleet Street. It is doubtful that Samuel Johnson spent any time here, but his chair and his parrot are displayed as evidence that he did. In any case, it is a fine example of a seventeenth-century tavern and very popular with the journalists of Fleet Street as well as with tourists. You would be well advised to go early, at 11.30, or late, at 2.30, but you can always crowd up to the bar for a drink.

A little further east on the north side of Fleet Street you will see signs directing you to Johnson's house, one of several that he lived in during his years in London. It is at No. 17 Gough Square and it is not always easy to find; either Johnson's Court or Bolt Court will lead you there. The house is open to visitors on weekdays and there is much interesting Johnson memorabilia inside, including several first editions of the famous Dictionary, which was put together on an upper floor with the help of several Scottish assistants.

Back once more to busy Fleet Street and, continuing eastward, you may want to take a brief look at St Bride's Church. It is just off Fleet Street, down a narrow entrance past Salisbury Court, on the south side of the street. This is another of Christopher Wren's reconstructions after the Great Fire, with a unique stepped-down tower. Tradition has it that the tower was visible to an eighteenth-century baker who had a shop nearby; the spire gave him the idea for creating stepped-down layers on wedding cakes.

A little further along Fleet Street you will find yourself at a busy intersection, Ludgate Circus; across the circus the street changes its name to Ludgate Hill and leads to St Paul's Cathedral. Wren wanted people to get a good view of the cathedral up this hill, but, unhappily, boxy office buildings have intervened. Walk just a short way up Ludgate Hill until you come to Old Bailey Street. If you turn left you will find the Old Bailey Criminal Courts on your right.

This is a massive new concrete structure built in the twentieth century. Newgate Prison stood on this corner for many years, holding many of England's most notorious criminals. They were regularly brought out for hanging, and St Sepulchre's Church, across the road, traditionally tolled its bells as the procession started westward on the long road to Tyburn.

The prison exists no longer, but criminals are still tried in the Central Criminal Court. As with the Royal Courts of Justice, you may visit a trial; the entrance is about halfway along. No cameras are allowed.

This is probably a good place to end such a long and complex walk. There are lots of buses at the top of Old Bailey, on Holborn Viaduct — here you are about three-quarters of a mile east of where we started. But there is a closer Underground station to your right, a short distance down Newgate Street — St Paul's — and there are other buses at Ludgate Circus.

Walk 9   *Embankment Mansions*   1 1/2 miles

Behold that narrow Street, which steep descends,
Whose Building to the slimy Shore extends . . .
There Essex' stately Pile adorn'd the Shore,
There Cecil's, Bedford's, Villers', now no more.
Yet Burlington's fair Palace still remains;
Beauty within, without Proportion reigns.

John Gay

THIS WALK will take you along the embankment, that
man-made river's edge created in the last half of the
nineteenth century to control the Thames, and up through
an area not far from Charing Cross that once was a place of
noble houses, each with a private river view and its own
landing stage.

We'll begin at Temple Underground station, easy to
reach because it is on both the District and Circle lines. This
is the boundary between Westminster and the City; when
you leave the station and walk out to the embankment you
should be able to find the stone griffins that are the symbol
of the City of London and that appear at many boundaries.

Our route will lead us up river towards Westminster. You
may wish to cross the road as soon as possible, so that you
can walk close to the river; there are many pleasant views.
There are also benches that invite you to a brief rest from
time to time and offer a chance to study the river activity in
comfort.

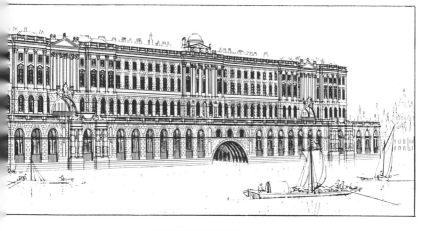

SOMERSET HOUSE

From here you can see across the river to the National Theatre with its moving electrical sign that announces current attractions. A little further on, after Waterloo Bridge, is the Royal Festival Hall. Just below you, before Waterloo Bridge, is the River Police Station; one of the small launches that regularly patrol the Thames may be moored there.

On the right as you walk along are a number of impressive buildings. The first ones you will see as you leave the station are the buildings of King's College of the University of London. The really monumental building that comes next is Somerset House, with its terrace built on a series of arches. It was begun as early as the sixteenth century, but was finished in the late eighteenth century. The large central arch was originally a water gate. Before the embankment was completed in the nineteenth century, the river extended far beyond its present banks. In fact, the principal street that parallels our route today, the Strand, suggests by its name that it was once the edge of the water.

83

After you walk beneath Waterloo Bridge, which carries both pedestrian and vehicular traffic, the river starts to make one of its many bends; soon, instead of running east and west, it will be running north and south. At Vauxhall Bridge, just beyond the Tate Gallery, it turns back again to its east–west direction. All of this meandering makes it difficult to define its banks by compass directions, but since its movement is generally east and west, we usually speak of the 'north' and 'south' sides.

Just after Waterloo Bridge you will pass Savoy Street; the large building is the Savoy Hotel and the Savoy Theatre. There have been historical buildings on this site since the thirteenth century. John of Gaunt lived in the Savoy Palace at one time; as one of the patrons of Geoffrey Chaucer he may well have entertained the poet here.

In more modern times, the Savoy Theatre is famous as the place where many Gilbert and Sullivan operettas were first performed, under the direction of Richard d'Oyly Carte, who gave his name to the company that produced those operettas for many years. The writers and director lived in this area and a little later we'll pass a pub that is called the Gilbert and Sullivan and that contains many mementoes to remind its patrons of those well-loved operettas.

At this point a pleasant park also appears on the right, Victoria Embankment Gardens. Savoy Place runs along the city side of these gardens, but we'll stay on the river's edge a little further, passing Cleopatra's Needle, the slender obelisk which is an Egyptian relic dating from about 1500 BC. You can read its history on the pedestal.

A little further along, just before we come to the Hungerford Foot Bridge, which runs beside the Charing Cross railway bridge, we'll turn away from the river on Villiers Street, in order to take a closer look at some of the embankment mansions — or at least what remains of them.

Villiers Street is named after George Villiers, the Duke of Buckingham, the friend and confidant of King James I and his son, Charles I, in the late sixteenth and early seventeenth centuries. Villiers was a proud man, not nobly born but achieving position through his personality and

YORK STAIRS

looks. It was his ambition to have a street named after each of his various names and titles in this area where he lived. He didn't quite achieve his aim, but this street bears his family name and a little later we'll pass one with his title, Buckingham. There was once a Duke Street and a George Street, but he probably never managed one named 'Of'.

A short distance up Villiers Street, just after you pass the boundary of Victoria Embankment Gardens, there is a set of steps going down to a narrow walkway, just beside a tiny building that leans precariously to the west. Down these steps to the left is a doorway without a sign, but it is the entrance to Gordon's Wine Bar, too popular to need any advertising. Inside, it is appropriately dark and cellar-like, but it serves a variety of interesting wines by the glass and bottle, as well as good meals. If it's lunch-time, this might be a place worth stopping.

On the right, off Villiers Street stands the Duke of Buckingham's water gate, a massive three-arch affair recently restored, all that remains of York House, built in the seventeenth century. The gate presently leads into the gardens; it once, of course, provided landing facilities for the duke's guests. There is a plaque attached that provides more information about the duke and his mansion.

Across from the water gate are steps leading up to Buckingham Street. Here you will find yourself once more isolated from the rushing traffic of the embankment below and the Strand above, in a little oasis of eighteenth-century houses, many of them almost unchanged. You'll see many such houses in the next few blocks of our walk, interspersed with modern office buildings; a number of the old houses carry blue plaques identifying former residents.

These houses are worth admiring for their architecture, not merely for the people who lived inside. Look particularly at the tall narrow windows, especially on the upper floors where the drawing-rooms and sitting-rooms were located. Also notice the fanlights, those semicircular windows above the door. Each one is a little different; they may have served to identify particular houses before numbering became popular. Finally, look for the extra flourishes, the wrought-iron work, including the cone-shaped torch snuffers at the doorway, the brackets for lamps and some of the balconies and grill work. These streets provide a wonderful example of the graceful, restrained domestic architecture of the eighteenth century.

At the top of Buckingham Street, turn right into John Adam Street. You are now in the area of the Adelphi, an extravagant series of town houses planned here on the riverside in the latter eighteenth century by the three Adam brothers, well-known architects of the time. The word Adelphi means 'brothers' in Greek, but it was an unlucky venture for the architects; because it was so expensive to build on the steep slope down to the river, the men spent all their money before they finished the project and they eventually went bankrupt. But the houses were completed and sold off by lottery.

The Adelphi was a popular if expensive place to live for at least a hundred years; some of the famous people who lived here are memorialized in blue plaques along the way. Though the planned community was torn down many years ago, isolated houses designed by the Adam brothers remain — you can see one of them in the distance at the very end of John Adam Street. Its narrow symmetrical shape was intended to be appreciated at this distance, but, when you get closer, you may appreciate some of the other marks of an Adam house, especially the decorative touches around the doors and windows.

As you walk up John Adam Street you will pass on the right one of the best of the Adam houses, now the home of the Royal Society of Arts. There is a plaque on the front of the building describing the functions of the society, which also dates back more than two hundred years. This whole area is very fascinating and there are many more discoveries to be made. You may wish to explore a few of the side streets on your own.

When you have seen enough, turn left at Adam Street (from John Adam Street, which might lead to confusion if you're not careful), and you will soon reach the Strand. This is a busy commercial street, noisy and full of traffic compared to the streets we have just left. Cross at the nearby pedestrian crossing and we will soon work our way back into a relatively quiet place, more appropriate for walkers.

First, though, if you look to the right, you should be able to see two fine churches built in the middle of this busy street. The first is St Mary-le-Strand, built by James Gibbs, one of Wren's pupils, who was also responsible for St Martin-in-the-Fields, near the National Gallery. The second church is St Clement Danes, one of Wren's own. This has the famous bells that ring out the first line of the nursery rhyme, 'Oranges and lemons, say the bells of St Clement's'. You can hear them four times a day, at nine, twelve, three and six o'clock. St Clement's is the official church of the Royal Air Force, and there is a special chapel inside dedicated to the men of the United States Eighth Air Force, who fought in Britain in the Second World War.

Once across the Strand, look for a narrow alleyway called Heathcock Court. It looks fairly unprepossessing, but it is a good pedestrian route north from the Strand. Walk along Heathcock Court, then Exchange Court, and in a short while you will be in Maiden Lane. Along the way notice the Dickensian gas lamps (still working) and appreciate the sense of an older time that has somehow remained down this dark alley—perhaps because it is too narrow for motor vehicles.

Maiden Lane is still a backwater, but a few yards on the right is a famous restaurant, Rule's, which is a good place for a splendid after-theatre dinner. Rule's is very English as far as its menu is concerned and very nineteenth century in its décor. Dickens was only one of many well-known people who frequented the place. Wealthy merchants, politicians and even royalty used to eat here.

We will go left along Maiden Lane, since continuing to the right would take us to Covent Garden and that is part of another walk. Today we will wander through a few more small and intriguing streets, eventually winding up in Leicester Square.

Turn back from Rule's and go along Maiden Lane until you come to Bedford Street, where you will turn right. You will pass Henrietta Street and then a narrow walkway called Inigo Place that will lead you into St Paul's Church, the actors' church, which is entered from this side but which has its most impressive façade on the opposite side, facing Covent Garden. The church is discussed in more detail in Walk No. 12.

Now continue along Bedford Street to the next major intersection, where King Street turns to the right. Across the way, angling up to the left, is Garrick Street. If you go up a few steps you will see Rose Street to the right. A few steps up Rose Street is the Lamb and Flag pub, favoured by literary people for centuries. Dryden was attacked outside the pub and severely beaten for some things he had written; no one has ever found out who was responsible, although there are plenty of theories. The Lamb and Flag is small, dark and smoky, but it has good English beer and cheese and continues to be popular at lunch-times.

Back down Rose Street and down Garrick Street, turning right at New Row, then left almost immediately and right again through a small archway, and you will find yourself in a really eighteenth-century lane. Goodwin's Court is only about twenty feet wide and perhaps a hundred yards long, but it has some of the finest old buildings, leaning a little now into the pavement, that you will see in all London.

These houses, each with a bulging bow window, are all now
made into offices. You can usually look in and see that the
interiors are all alike, and all typical: they contain a very
small room with a narrow stairway at the right leading to the
upper floors. Such a place is a decorator's dream, and all the
office holders seem to be in competition with one another to
achieve the most eighteenth-century interior. Not too many
people find Goodwin's Court, fortunately, or the
secretaries inside would probably start to feel persecuted by
everyone peering in at the windows.

Goodwin's Court leads, too soon, to busy St Martin's
Lane, in the midst of the entertainment district, but there is
one more quiet pedestrian walk before we finish. Almost
directly across St Martin's Lane is Cecil Court, a little wider,
not quite so authentic, but still interesting. It is a short
street, almost completely occupied by secondhand
bookshops. A bibliophile could spend a lifetime here,
admiring, touching, sometimes even buying.

But we are now at the end of this walk. Cecil Court will
lead you to Charing Cross Road and just beyond is Leicester
Square, where you might like to stop at the half-price ticket
booth to pick up seats for tonight's play. Leicester Square
Underground station is just up Charing Cross Road to the
right, and there are many buses in both directions. We are
back now in the busy world of the twentieth century.

O ye associate Walkers, O my Friends,
Upon your State what Happiness attends!

John Gay

IN THIS walk we'll encounter London at its oldest and most
venerable, and also at its newest and most innovative.
Along the way we'll see a good bit of both economic and
ecclesiastical history, as we visit markets and guilds, an
ancient chapel, London's oldest hospital and some
beautiful old churches. This will be a mixed sightseeing
tour, with something to interest everyone.

We begin at the Chancery Lane Underground station
(District line) or, if it is more convenient, Holborn (District
and Piccadilly lines), which will add about a quarter of a
mile to the walk.

At the Chancery Lane station you are right at the
boundary of the City of London; if you come above ground
on the north side of Holborn you will see several stone
pillars nearby as markers. The walk today will be largely
along this northern boundary, in and out of the old City,
with a glimpse at the end of surviving parts of the old City
wall.

But the most interesting thing to be seen at this beginning
of the walk is the handsome gabled and half-timbered
building on the south side of Holborn at this point. This is
Staple Inn, which dates from 1586 when it was an Inn of
Chancery, a residence and school for lawyers. It has literary
associations also — Dr Johnson lived here for a time and
wrote his only novel, *Rasselas*, in this building.

90

STAPLE INN, HOLBORN

The inn presently serves as offices and consists of two small quadrangles. Cross the street; in about the middle of the façade you will find a small archway that will lead you into the first courtyard and then on to the second, which includes a pleasant garden, unfortunately not open to the public. But this is too early in the walk to be searching for a place to rest.

Cross Holborn to the north side again and continue north, away from the noise and traffic, along Brooke Street. This little street is not much to look at today, but it is rich in literary associations: in 1770, Thomas Chatterton, the 'marvellous boy' who faked some delightful medieval poems, committed suicide in a rented room here, and the huge red brick building on the right is where Furnival's Inn once stood, where Charles Dickens lived when he wrote the first part of *Pickwick Papers*.

But these modern commercial buildings show little sign of their fascinating past, so we'll continue. Turn right at the first corner, into Greville Street, and the atmosphere immediately changes; once more you are in a street of small shops, similar to the ones that must have been here a century or more ago. Soon you will come to Hatton Gardens. Here you are in the centre of the thriving diamond trade — almost every shop offers jewellery and gems for

91

sale. Prices are often good too, because these merchants do not pay the high rents of Piccadilly and St James's.

Turn right at Hatton Gardens, back towards Holborn, and stay on the left side of the street, looking for a small passageway called Ely Court which will lead to a remarkably well-preserved eighteenth-century tavern called the Mitre Inn. The rather gaudily painted bishop's mitre above the door will remind you that you are now entering an area that centuries ago provided the town residence of the Bishops of Ely.

The only remnant of the bishop's palace is the marvellous St Etheldreda's Chapel, just around the corner to the left in Ely Place. Go in and visit both the crypt, which is built on Roman foundations, and the beautiful chapel itself, with its old wooden roof and modern stained glass and statues of martyrs. The chapel was built in the late thirteenth century.

After leaving the chapel, go back the way you came along Ely Place down to a major intersection, Holborn Circus. Directly across is the church of St Andrew, Holborn. Like many other City churches, St Andrew's was rebuilt by Christopher Wren in the late seventeenth century, even though it was not burned in the Great Fire. It was, however, severely damaged in the bombing of the Second World War, but it has been largely restored to its original form today. Since it no longer serves an active parish, it is not open at weekends.

The reason that St Andrew's is no longer an active parish church is easy to see when you stand outside. Once it was surrounded by small buildings where people lived and worked, but now it is totally surrounded by high-rise office buildings.

St Andrew's sits peacefully on this busy commercial corner, up till now resisting the ever-present pressure of developers. Like many other small churches that you will pass on these walks, it provides a quiet and restful haven from the bustling noise and frenetic activity outside; it is always a good place to sit and rest and ponder the passage of time.

But now it's back to those busy streets once more, to investigate some of the commercial activity that dominates this area. Cross back to Charter House Street that runs north-east from Holborn Circus. Soon Charter House Street will cross Farringdon Road, and, as you cross, you might glance at the small statue of a griffin that stands in the middle of the street on the right. This is another one of the markers, using the City of London symbol, that define the boundaries of the City. We're now just outside those precincts.

Continue along Charter House Street and you will see in front of you the long low buildings that are Smithfield Market, the wholesale meat market of London. If you arrive before noon you will still find some activity — a few people hauling sides of beef or whole lamb carcasses — but the real action takes place at dawn or even earlier. Originally simply a 'Smooth Field' just outside the City walls and thus a place for exhibitions and communal activities, it has been the site of tournaments, a place of execution and the site of the famous Bartholomew Fair.

As you walk up Charter House Street almost to the end of the expanse of the market, you will see an aptly named street on your left, Cowcross Street. It is now a street of interesting small shops and restaurants, but in your imagination you may see cows being driven to market. Up until the middle of the last century, horses and cattle were sold at Smithfield Market as well as sides of beef; they were driven through the city streets, frequently clogging up the traffic.

Continue up to the end of the market, and then follow Charter House Street as it turns left, leading to a pleasant green space, Charterhouse Square. On the left of the square you can see the original gatehouse to the ancient monastery which gave the place its name. Founded in the fourteenth century, the Charterhouse has been endowed as a home for indigent gentlemen since 1611 — residents have to have been professional men or officers in the army or navy — and as a public school for boys. The school has turned out some famous men — Addison and Steele, the eighteenth-century essayists, and John Wesley, founder of Methodism — but it has since been moved to the country. This location is still a residence for old gentlemen and hence is not open to the

ST BARTHOLOMEW THE GREAT

public, but the gateway can be examined from the square.

After a rest in the square, return the way you came to the market. On your way you may notice a pub with remarkable opening hours — from 6.30 to 9 in the morning. This is, of course, to accommodate the market people, who have been working most of the night. You may also notice, as you continue, that many of the restaurants in the area are open chiefly for breakfast. Here time is a little reversed.

When you come back to the market buildings, walk to the left or south side to Long Lane. Before you have gone very far you will catch a glimpse through a narrow passageway of another church. This is St Bartholomew the Great, one of London's oldest churches, which is well worth a visit.

Walk through the passageway and among the

gravestones until you find the three or four steps that lead down to the entrance to the church. Some parts of St Bartholomew go as far back as 1123 and the history of its founding is fascinating to read; there are inexpensive pamphlets available at a small bookstall inside. Be sure to visit the old cloister to your right as you enter the church, as well as the church itself. The Lady Chapel, which has been largely rebuilt from its original form, was once a printing shop; Benjamin Franklin worked there for a while. There is much more to be seen; you may wish to spend some time here or come back at another time, perhaps for a Sunday service.

When you leave, do not go back the way you came, but continue straight ahead, along what was once the aisle of the nave and through the archway in the building in front of you, which was once the main entrance to the church. After you have come out, cross the narrow street and then look back at the fine half-timbering on the house. Interestingly enough, this was revealed only in 1915, when a Zeppelin bomb during the First World War dislodged some tiles that had covered up the half-timbering for many years.

In front of you now as you continue is St Bartholomew's Hospital. It was established by the same man who endowed the church you have just visited, a man obviously concerned with both body and soul. Both church and hospital go back to the early twelfth century, although the buildings of the hospital are much newer. But a hospital has been on this site for all this time and now it has become famous as a teaching hospital. Its chief physician in the early seventeenth century was William Harvey, the first person to demonstrate the circulation of the blood.

Inside the grounds, on your left, is a small church, St Bartholomew the Less, the parish church for the hospital only. It has an unusual octagonal shape and is worth a look. Inside the second courtyard are the main buildings of the hospital, most of them designed by the eighteenth-century architect, James Gibbs, whose work we have seen elsewhere on these walks.

Outside the hospital once more, as you continue down Giltspur Street, you will pass Cock Lane on the right, a small street with an interesting history. If you look up you will see on the building on the near corner the small gilt statue of a naked boy; this is 'Pye Corner' and the little boy is supposed to mark the place where the Great Fire of 1666 finally stopped. The boy is grossly fat — as if he had eaten too many pies. Many people considered the destructive fire God's judgement on the sinful people who lived in its path, especially the gluttonous, since the fire began in Pudding Lane and ended at Pye Corner. In fact, the fire burned further, but the story is still a good one.

It was also in Cock Lane, in 1762, that a young girl claimed to have contact with a ghost. She was widely believed and people claimed to have heard night-time knockings and scratchings near her bed. Dr Johnson was one of a number of learned and scientific people who sat by her bed most of one night to put an end to the stories. But Cock Lane itself is now a ghost, as all the houses where these events took place have been torn down for office buildings.

Giltspur Street ends at Newgate Street, at the famous corner which was the site of Newgate Prison, the place from which many prisoners began their last long ride to the gallows at Tyburn. The present buildings are not a prison but the Central Criminal Courts of London (see Walk No. 8).

We'll turn left on Newgate Street, past the main post office building (not for the general public — for that you need to go up King Edward Street, just beyond) and the Postal Museum, with its amazingly comprehensive collection of the world's stamps. Cross over the major intersection, St Martin-le-Grand, and turn left at the next, smaller street, Foster Lane. Almost immediately on your left you'll see the basement location of an old tavern, now called the London Pipe, a pleasant wine bar which is a popular place with local businessmen and women.

A little further down Foster Lane, on the right at Gresham Street, is an ornate building, Goldsmith's Hall, home of one of the City's richest guilds. It is not open to the public except on special occasions, but if you crane your neck from across the street you should be able to see some of the elaborate chandeliers on the first floor.

Turn right down Gresham Street and you will find

yourself very soon at St Lawrence Jewry, the very large and luxurious City church. You may want to walk in and admire its spaciousness and sumptuous furnishings.

When you come out, walk around the church to the east end, which is really the front, and you will be in the courtyard of the Guildhall, the headquarters for the collective organization of all the City guilds, in effect the centre of administrative control for the City. Inside is the Great Hall, which is used for various ceremonial meetings including the annual Lord Mayor's banquet. Notice particularly the giant carved wood figures of Gog and Magog above the entrance. These were carved after the Second World War, when the Guildhall roof and much of the interior was destroyed by fire, but they replace similar figures that had been there for centuries.

You may also want to visit the Guildhall Library, the modern building just west of the Guildhall, with its entrance on Aldermanbury Street. It houses a splendid collection of materials on London history as well as a collection of clocks, chronometers and other time-keeping instruments maintained by the Clockmaker's Company. Upstairs there is a library of maps and a place to get many free pamphlets on London history as well as inexpensive reproductions of old maps and prints and even playing cards and greeting cards.

From the Guildhall Library, take Love Lane (once a street of prostitutes) west to Wood Street, then right (north) to London Wall, not a wall today but a broad avenue that runs roughly along the route of the old City wall. Turn left at London Wall and then right when you see the sign for the London Museum, which will guide you up some steps to the pedestrian area of the Barbican where we'll finish this walk.

The Barbican is a city within the City. Thousands of people live within the four tall residential towers and thousands more come for the many performances that take place here. The Museum of London is only one of many reasons to visit the Barbican; it offers a compelling and comprehensive history of the settlement and growth of London, from prehistoric through Roman times up to the mid-twentieth century. It is built on the site of the old City wall, and excavated parts of that wall, seen through

97

windows, are incorporated as an exhibit. The museum deserves at least a half-day of your time — but probably not today at the end of this fairly long walk.

From the museum you can follow the yellow lines painted on the ground to the Barbican Centre where, among other things, you can pick up printed materials describing current exhibitions and performances. You can also orient yourself to all the delights the centre has to offer.

The Barbican is the London home of the Royal Shakespeare Company. It operates two theatres, one large one that offers plays of Shakespeare and other classical writers, sometimes including performances that are brought down from Stratford, and a small theatre that offers new and experimental productions. There is also a film theatre, a concert hall, a library, several galleries, three or four restaurants and numerous bars.

The whole complex is difficult to describe, difficult even to comprehend on your first visit. It is perhaps too big, not quite human in size, and thus easy to get lost in; people who come here to go to a play sometimes wander around looking for the theatre until the last act. It's wise to scout out the territory in advance — and allow extra time.

For today, it is a good place to finish a walk, because you can walk around at your leisure and perhaps find a bar or a restaurant for a cup of coffee or a drink, while you read some of the literature you have picked up along the way. Later, you will want to return for a play or a concert, a visit to the museum or one of the galleries.

When you are ready to leave, you have a variety of choices and there are lots of signs that point the way. Three Underground stations are nearby: Barbican, with the Metropolitan and District lines on the north-west corner; Moorgate, with those two lines plus the Northern on the eastern side; and St Paul's, about a quarter of a mile to the south, which is on the Central line. In addition, there are a number of buses on Aldersgate Street to the west and Moorgate to the east. Of course if your feet are tired after all this exploration, there are likely to be taxis to take you swiftly and comfortably and not too expensively to wherever you wish to go.

If drawn by Bus'ness to a Street unknown,
Let the sworn Porter point thee through the Town;
Be sure observe the Signs, for Signs remain,
Like faithful Land-marks to the walking Train.
Seek not from Prentices to learn the Way,
Those fabling Boys will turn thy Steps astray;
Ask the grave Tradesman to direct thee right,
He ne'er deceives, but when he profits by't.

John Gay

THE EPIGRAPH for today's walk gives good advice in general for any walk, but it may be especially applicable to this walk, for we will spend our time away from principal avenues while we explore narrow lanes and back streets, often with unexpected twists and turns.

Bloomsbury, the area we will explore today, grew up as the aristocrats of the eighteenth century fled the areas of trade and commerce to build their homes in the country. The green and pleasant squares that we will pass still bear their names: Bedford, Russell, Gordon, Brunswick, even if they no longer include their houses. For, as London expanded, trade and commerce followed, and the aristocracy were driven still further out of the city.

Bloomsbury became rather dilapidated and run-down by the end of the last century and was therefore less fashionable. Since that time its reputation has come to depend not on the aristocracy but on its intellectuals, for both the British Museum and London University have come to dominate the area. In the period after the First

World War, the area became the haunt of the small and eccentric group of writers and intellectuals who came to be known as the 'Bloomsbury Group' — Virginia and Leonard Woolf, Clive and Vanessa Bell, Lytton Strachey and E.M. Forster.

Along the course of this walk, we will have quite a lot to look out for — the remnants of former grandeur, signs of encroaching trade, evidence of distinguished intellectuals in the British Museum and London University, as well as several small specialized galleries and museums. It will indeed be necessary to 'observe the Signs'.

We start this time at St Giles Circus, a major intersection of Oxford Street and Charing Cross Road. The Underground station is called Tottenham Court Road, which is on the District and Northern lines, and there are plenty of buses from every point of the compass.

This is the place at which Oxford Street from the west becomes New Oxford Street to the east, and Charing Cross Road from the south becomes Tottenham Court Road to the north. Here we will find heavy traffic and a great number of shops, but we will soon walk into calmer and quieter areas. Start north at Tottenham Court Road, on the east side, and pass the first road, Great Russell Street, which would lead directly to the British Museum, and take the second, Bedford Avenue, which, if you turn left, will lead to Bedford Square.

Bedford Square has suffered less from modern rebuilding than most of the squares in this area. As you walk around you will see eighteenth-century houses, many of them much as they were — at least from the outside — several hundred years ago. This is a good introduction to Bloomsbury, because it gives an early glimpse of what the whole area used to be like; the appearance of the houses here will help you to identify the remnants of grandeur that you will find elsewhere.

Leave Bedford Square on Bloomsbury Street and you will see the massive building of the British Museum on your left. Follow it around along Great Russell Street to the main entrance. The British Museum is one of the greatest museums in the world and certainly deserves a separate day of exploration at least, so we will not talk much about it here. As an institution, it was founded in the mid-eighteenth century, with the nucleus of its collection being that of Sir Hans Sloane (see Walk No. 18). It moved to this location in the early nineteenth century, although the great columns and the central façade that you can see through the railings from Great Russell Street were not completed till the mid-nineteenth century.

The British Museum is in some ways two separate institutions: a museum of antiquities for the general public as well as for scholars, and a library just for scholars. The library is the official repository for every printed book produced in Britain and many of those produced elsewhere in the world; its collection of historical books and documents is one of the world's greatest. The famous circular reading room in the centre of the building has been the office and study for many important scholars and still is a magnet that draws academics to its collections; Karl Marx wrote *Das Kapital* at one of its desks. If you demonstrate a serious purpose and can show a letter of introduction, you may be granted a reader's card.

The museum collection is too extensive for brief description, but we will mention three outstanding items studied by thousands of visitors every month. In the Duveen Gallery, you will find the remarkable sculptures from the Greek Parthenon known as the Elgin Marbles, so named because they were acquired in the early nineteenth century by the Seventh Earl of Elgin. One of the splendid Egyptian rooms, which are filled with monumental sculpture, houses the Rosetta Stone, the all-important discovery that prints an ancient decree in three languages and thus provides the key to Egyptian hieroglyphics. And in the manuscript collection are two of the four surviving copies of Magna Carta, as well as the Shakespeare Deed, containing one of the few authenticated signatures of the playwright.

If these things and thousands more like them interest you, you will wish to return to the British Museum again and again. But for today we will simply walk past the façade, perhaps making a note that across the street is the delightful old Museum Tavern, with its stained glass, huge mirrors and velvet curtains — always a haunt of scholars.

For now, let's continue east along Great Russell Street, which will lead shortly to Bloomsbury Square on the right. This is one of the oldest squares in the area; a quick walk around will show some remnants of the ancient past. Or, since we will be seeing lots of such squares today, you may wish to move directly north from here along the broad and pleasant Bedford Place, which leads to Russell Square.

Russell Square shares with Lincoln's Inn Fields the distinction of being one of the largest squares in Central London. It is surrounded by small and large hotels, many of them quite inexpensive, appropriate for impecunious scholars who wish to work at the British Museum or enrol at London University. There is also a statue of the Duke of Bedford on the south side of the square, the man who gave his name to so many of the places we have seen — his family name was Russell.

Because Russell Square is so large and green, you may like to walk through it; if you do, turn to the right when you first face the square, and walk through it diagonally from the south-eastern to the north-western corner, because it is from the latter point that the walk will continue. Or if you walk up the west side of the square, you will see some of the principal buildings of London University on your left.

London University is a relative newcomer to the British system of higher education. Established early in the nineteenth century, it has none of the ancient traditions of Oxford and Cambridge, but it has already made a name for itself in the quality and scope of its courses and the size of its student body. It has also the distinction of being the first of the major British universities to grant admission to women — more than a hundred years ago. It consists not of one campus but many, and its various colleges and professional schools can be found all over central London. These buildings to the west of Russell Square are, however, the administrative centre.

From the north-west corner of Russell Square we will continue north just a short distance to Woburn Square, which is not a square at all but a pair of streets divided by a

102

narrow green park. On the north-west corner of Woburn Square are the Courtauld Institute Galleries, which are part of the university.

The Courtauld Galleries seem to be a surprisingly well-kept secret; you will rarely find the crowds of visitors here that you find at other better-known London art galleries. Yet the quality is magnificent, particularly the collection of French Impressionist and Post-Impressionist paintings, whose donor, Samuel Courtauld, gave the gallery its name. There are also good examples of early Italian art and a fine collection of old master drawings. If you should find yourself spending so much time here that you do not want to complete the walk, Russell Square Underground station is just off the north-east corner of the square and Euston Square station is just to the north along Euston Road.

But if you do wish to continue the walk, we'll move next along the south side of Gordon Square. Gordon Square saw the beginning of the Bloomsbury Group, at the home of Virginia Woolf, No. 46; Lytton Strachey and Clive Bell also lived in the square. And at the south-east corner, No. 53, you'll find another little-known London art gallery, the Percival David Foundation of Chinese Art, which has an excellent collection of Chinese ceramics. Stop here for a brief look if you like, but we still have some other interesting places to visit.

To the east and north of Gordon Square is Tavistock Square. Work your way around these squares to the north-east corner of Tavistock Square and continue north along Woburn Place. If you turn right before you get to busy Euston Road, on Woburn Walk, you will find yourself in a delightful short street with original eighteenth-century shop fronts. Here is an example of the trade that followed the wealthy home-owners.

The small shops continue to the left, along Duke's Street, if you want to take a brief detour, but we'll be making our way east and south now to the very large expanse of green on your map which is identified as Coram Fields, with a western extension taking in Brunswick Square and an eastern extension called Mecklenburgh Square. There are many small streets you may take here; perhaps this is a good place to allow each walker to 'observe the Signs' and proceed at his or her own pace, by whatever route seems easy, to the northern side of Brunswick Square.

Here we are looking for Coram House, which we will find at No. 40 Brunswick Square. It looks like an ordinary residence, but it is the museum of the Coram Foundation, so walk up the steps and enter for another fascinating view of eighteenth-century life.

Thomas Coram was a philanthropist who started a hospital for foundlings — abandoned children. He built a school and trained them for useful work. The school no longer exists — it stood in Coram Fields — but the foundation that he endowed still operates from Coram House, which has become a museum.

Much of the interior remains as it was in the eighteenth century when Thomas Coram lived here, and the museum contains fascinating memorabilia of the children and of the patrons who helped to support the hospital. One such benefactor was the painter Hogarth; you can see his portrait of Thomas Coram here. Another was the musician Handel; there is a manuscript score of his *Messiah* on view as well as the organ that he used to play. You may also want to look at some of the 'tokens' that were left for identification purposes with the abandoned infants — these all make for a fascinating exhibit.

Leaving Coram House, walk south around Brunswick Square and then along the south side of Coram Fields (which is a playground for children); continue east along Guildford Street almost as far as Gray's Inn Road. But turn right along Doughty Street just before, and on your left you will find one of the houses that Dickens lived in, now an important Dickens museum.

Dickens lived here while he wrote some of his most important novels, *Oliver Twist* and *Nicholas Nickleby*, and the museum contains much manuscript material, a number of letters and all kinds of other memorabilia. You can find traces of Dickens all over London, but this museum has the most abundant and authentic material.

Finally, we'll continue south down Doughty Street,

FRANCIS BACON

which becomes John Street, to one last green space, Gray's Inn. In a previous walk (No. 8) we saw three Inns of Court, places of education for lawyers. Gray's Inn is the fourth and only other such Inn that operated in London in past centuries — its most famous graduate was Francis Bacon, who lived here for almost fifty years until his death in 1626; his statue stands in South Square and he is generally credited with laying out the extensive gardens in the north.

Those gardens may or may not be open to pedestrians, depending upon the time of day. If they are, stroll through them, leaving to the south by way of Fulwood Place, which will lead you to High Holborn, perhaps with a stop to visit the Chapel and the Hall, both built in the sixteenth century, largely destroyed in 1941, but since restored. If the gardens are closed, you will have to go along to Gray's Inn Road and follow that south to Holborn.

By either route, you should soon find yourself at Chancery Lane Underground, where the District line will take you east or west, and on Holborn, with bus lines that spread to all corners of London. You will be back in a busy business area, away from the aristocratic and intellectual delights of the fascinating area known as Bloomsbury.

Soho, Leicester Square, Covent Garden

Where Covent-garden's famous Temple stands,
That boasts the Work of Jones' immortal Hands;
Columns, with plain Magnificence, appear,
And graceful Porches lead along the Square:
Here oft' my Course I bend . . .

John Gay

THIS WALK might well be titled 'Eating and Entertainment in Central London', for all varieties of those activities will be found along the way. But the area is a strange one: at the beginning of the seventeenth century it was an early expansion of the City westward, a place where wealthy men built country estates. Since then all the commercial activities of the inner city have so thoroughly swallowed it up that it has become a little seedy and run-down. Perhaps its most remarkable quality is the wide range of experiences that can be found here — everything from the cheapest snack bars to the most expensive continental restaurants, from strip shows to the best of London theatre and opera.

We'll begin once more at Piccadilly Circus, an area that epitomizes that extreme range of possibilities, for, as every walker soon discovers, Piccadilly Circus can change from dignified to dilapidated within a few steps. We'll start walking up Shaftesbury Avenue, named after the philanthropic earl who is also honoured by the sculpture of the Angel of Charity in the middle.

On the north side of Shaftesbury Avenue you will find four well-known theatres, all of them regularly showing excellent plays — the Lyric, Apollo, Globe and Queen's. It is always interesting to look at the photographs of the productions displayed outside and to read the glowing encomiums of critics that the managements choose to exhibit. The box offices are usually open during the day, so that you can reserve a seat for a future performance of any play that takes your fancy.

But the contrast continues. If you had turned up Great Windmill Street, just short of these theatres, you would have seen a pornographic film theatre on the left and the famous Windmill Theatre on the right, which for years has shown mildly erotic films or stage presentations. The Windmill Theatre asserts proudly that it has never closed, even during the blitz of London in the Second World War — a patriotic gesture, as the girls risked life and limb to entertain the boys back from the Front.

If you turn left, or north from Shaftesbury Avenue along Rupert Street and follow it until it becomes Berwick Street, you will find yourself in the midst of another contrast. Berwick Street is lined with little strip shows on both sides, but down the centre of the road is a charming fruit and vegetable market, with a great number of small stands selling excellent and cheap produce. If hunger attacks, you can buy an apple or a bunch of grapes.

Berwick Street eventually leads to Oxford Street, but before you go that far turn right down any one of the small streets and venture along to Soho Square. Along the way you'll cross Wardour Street and Dean Street; both are lined with restaurants of varying price and quality. All of them display their menus outside — reading menus can be almost as fascinating as looking at theatre posters. You will find here many small Chinese restaurants, for we are not far from the centre of London's Chinatown.

The area we are in is known as Soho; probably called this after the hunting cry that resounded through the air when this place was largely green fields. Whatever its origin, the name has stuck over the years. So has its reputation, for over the years Soho has been noted for entertainment that the guidebooks describe as 'of a dubious nature'. It was for a long time the home of prostitutes and may still be, although they will not force themselves on your attention, for the police are strict about soliciting.

But Soho was also once an area of aristocratic residences, most of which have since disappeared or have been so altered as to be unrecognizable. Still, if you have done enough walking by this time to recognize some of the qualities of an eighteenth-century house, you may find a few around here. One of the best-known early occupants of Soho Square was the Duke of Monmouth, an illegitimate son of Charles II (he had many) who led a revolt against his father and was later executed. The revolt is recorded in Dryden's long poem, 'Absalom and Achitophel'. Mozart lived here too and gave music lessons in a house on Soho Square.

Today, the square is rather prosaic, with offices of people in the music business and restaurants. Nor is it risky to walk around here, as it would have been several hundred years ago. Soho Square is pleasantly green and attractive; the whole area may be a little seedy but it is not dangerous.

When you have seen enough of the square, leave to the south, down Greek Street, and head towards Leicester Square. Greek Street offers more restaurants, often small and of high quality. If it is lunch-time, this might be the place to pause.

Just before you cross Shaftesbury Avenue again, you will see on your left the bulk of the Palace Theatre; it faces Charing Cross Road at Cambridge Circus. We are in the heart of the theatre district. The Phoenix Theatre is a short distance north on Charing Cross Road; to the south, on Charing Cross Road and St Martin's Lane, there are at least a dozen more important theatres.

Rather than walk along the busy thoroughfare, however, you will probably find it more interesting to continue along some of Soho's smaller streets on your way to Leicester Square. Cross Shaftesbury Avenue down Newport Place — the continuation of Greek Street — and turn right into Gerrard Street. You'll find lots of Chinese restaurants and supermarkets here; during the Chinese New Year celebration in the spring, the streets will be packed with revellers.

Continue down Gerrard Street to Wardour Street, turn left and you will soon be in Leicester Square, a fashionable new residential area in the eighteenth century, today the busy centre of London's entertainment industry. Jonathan Swift had rooms here, so did William Hogarth and Sir Joshua Reynolds. Dr Burney, the eighteenth-century music historian and critic, lived in St Martin's Street, just south, and his more famous daughter, Fanny, wrote her best-known novel, *Evelina*, in that house — it's now the Westminster Reference Library.

Leicester Square is not the quiet green garden that so many London squares are; in the summer the whole surface comes alive with the multitude of people who fill it. In the centre, if you can find it, is a statue of Shakespeare, incongruous at first glance, but as Shakespeare was a popular entertainer he ought to be comfortable in the midst of all the variety offered here.

Most of the square is now surrounded by large cinemas, playing the most popular of current films; eighty years ago those same theatres were music halls, providing that uniquely British form of entertainment which is remembered now with nostalgia and sometimes revived. Restaurants, pubs and snack bars seem to fill the rest of Leicester Square, and always people of all kinds. While most of these walks call your attention to buildings, this walk is ideal for people-watching; you will find plenty of subjects at Leicester Square and later at Covent Garden.

When you leave Leicester Square, walk east from the north-east corner along either Cranbourn Street or — if you can find it — tiny Bear Street. Both will lead you to Charing Cross Road and to more theatres — Wyndham's and the Albery, the Garrick and Duke of York's to the south.

Go from Charing Cross Road to St Martin's Lane down St Martin's Court, then continue east on New Row, a narrow street with a number of fascinating small shops and small restaurants. At Bedford Street, turn right for a short walk to Inigo Place, which will lead you to St Paul's Church — not the cathedral but one of three or four London churches with this name.

St Paul's Church was designed by Inigo Jones in the 1630s, and built as an integral part of Covent Garden, which it faces on the east. It has come to be known as the 'Actors' Church', partly because it is in the middle of the theatre district and also because so many actors are buried or memorialized here. Inside you should be able to identify the names of many, from Dame Ellen Terry to Vivien Leigh.

Other well-known people are connected with the church, too. William Wycherley, the eighteenth-century playwright, is buried here, the painter J.M.W. Turner was baptized here and so was W.S. Gilbert, the comic poet who collaborated with Sir Arthur Sullivan in so many light operas. If you look around, you will probably find other names you recognize.

The church itself is rather beautiful and much larger than most parish churches. There is a story told about its design: the Earl of Bedford had spent so much money in laying out the residential square in Covent Garden that he needed to economize on the church that was to fill its fourth side. He reportedly advised Inigo Jones simply to build a 'big barn'. Jones complied and provided the Duke with the world's most beautiful barn.

When you have finished examining St Paul's, you can leave the churchyard to the north, into King Street, which will lead you around to the front of the church and Covent Garden, another good area for people-watching. You can never be sure what you will find, particularly in the open area between the church portico and the entrance to the covered shopping area. Sometimes there are mimes, or jugglers, or a Punch and Judy show — you may even see a flower seller who looks like Eliza Doolittle, for it was in this area that Professor Higgins met the cockney girl whose life he transformed by changing her accent in Shaw's *Pygmalion*, and in the musical stage adaptation, *My Fair Lady*.

Covent Garden is a corruption of the name Convent Garden; the area was owned by the monks of Westminster as early as the thirteenth century. In the seventeenth

century the site was developed into splendid town houses by the Earl of Bedford, with fine arched walkways around three sides and the church on the fourth. In the late eighteenth century the area became the haunt of writers and artists, who spent much time in the numerous coffee houses in the area.

In addition, from very early on, the centre of the square became a fruit, vegetable and flower market, the largest in London. That activity continued until 1974, when the market was moved to the outskirts of London; since then, the covered market area has been rebuilt into a shopping mall, with many small shops and a number of pleasant restaurants and pubs. The centre of the market area is usually filled with the stalls of craftspeople selling their wares.

Remnants of all this history can be seen wherever you look. Covent Garden will reward a lengthy visit. Among other things, you may wish to look in on the Transport Museum on the east side, which contains examples of some of London's earliest omnibuses, coaches and Underground trains. There is a fascinating exhibit on the growth and

BOW STREET AND POLICE

operation of the London Underground, as well as a convincing explanation — which nobody believes — of how the London buses are spaced evenly on their route. This is another excellent place to spend a rainy afternoon.

We'll make a further brief excursion east before we end this walk, to identify a few other interesting places. When you leave the square to go east down Russell Street the first road you cross is Bow Street (named because of its gently curving shape). On the corner here once stood the bookshop of Tom Davies, where Boswell was first introduced to Johnson. Along Bow Street to the left is the Bow Street Police Station, where Henry Fielding the novelist and his blind brother John were magistrates; they established the 'Bow Street Runners' who were the forerunners of the modern police plain-clothes detectives.

Across the street from the police station is the Royal Opera House, home of the Royal Ballet and Opera. Built in the mid-nineteenth century, it has a most impressive exterior with its huge columns; the interior is equally grand, with seating for more than 2000 people, a grand staircase and red velvet curtains with gold embroidery.

A little further along Russell Street, at the corner of Catherine Street, is the Drury Lane Theatre, the old Theatre Royal that housed the 'King's Company' in the late seventeenth century, which had Charles II as royal patron. In the eighteenth century David Garrick was the manager here and the opening night prologue was written by his friend Samuel Johnson, which included the famous lines about the acting profession, 'We that live to please must please to live.'

The original building burned down and it has been rebuilt a number of times; perhaps the most famous conflagration was in 1809 when the playwright Richard Brinsley Sheridan was manager. Having decided that the fire was out of control, and knowing that he would be bankrupt, he sat in a nearby tavern and ordered a bottle of wine. When someone asked how he could be so calm, he replied, 'Cannot a man enjoy a glass of wine by his own fireside?'

This seems like a good place to end this walk, with the recollection of all the famous actors who performed at the Drury Lane Theatre, whose paintings and statues can be seen in the lobby, and also the currently well-known actors who are now playing at the theatres we have passed today. The theatrical tradition of London is long and enduring; when walking wears you out, the theatre will give you new vitality.

When you are ready to head for home, the Covent Garden Underground is just north of the market area, along Long Acre. If you walk south down any of these streets you will soon find yourself in the Strand, not far from Charing Cross, where there is another Underground Station, as well as plenty of buses.

Christopher Wren
and Parish Churches   1 ¹/₂ miles

> Sir Christopher Wren
> Said, 'I am going to dine with some men.
> If anybody calls
> Say I'm designing St Paul's.'

Edmund Clerihew Bentley

THIS WALK will lead you to a dozen parish churches in the City of London, all of them intriguing for different reasons, most of them designed by the great seventeenth-century architect, Christopher Wren. Wren's architectural talents may have surprised even him — he was trained as a mathematician and astronomer — but after the Great Fire of 1666 that destroyed most of central London, he rose to the challenge and designed more than fifty churches, as well as the great cathedral of St Paul's.

Many of these churches were damaged severely in the bombing of the Second World War, but most of them have since been rebuilt, in some cases closer to Wren's original intention than they were before the bombing, for many alterations had been made during the nineteenth century when a neo-Gothic style was popular. This Gothicism, with its dark woodwork and quantities of stained glass, was quite opposed to Wren's intention.

Wren's churches emphasize a true congregation of worshippers, all prepared to take an active part in the service, to be more than spectators. To further this end, he liked clear glass, for lots of light, and cheerful pastel colours, blue, grey and rose, with white and gold decorative touches. Services in a Wren church emphasize the brotherhood of man rather than the mysteries of God, the

Sr. Wren

power of reason rather than the force of faith, appropriate attitudes for the time in which he lived and still appealing to many contemporary religious people.

Whatever your own religious beliefs, you will find some of these Wren interiors worthy of study. You do not need to go inside all these churches — indeed, some may be closed for one reason or another — but you should look at a few so that you can get a sense of the use of space that is typical of a Wren design, as well as a sense of the great range of his imagination. This walk will mention only a few details of each church; you will usually be able to pick up a printed brochure inside that will provide additional information.

You will sometimes find a verger present, happy to answer questions, pleased that a visitor has shown an interest in the church. Don't forget to deposit a small contribution in the usually inconspicuous offering box towards building maintenance — it takes a lot of money to keep these old churches in repair and, in the centre of the City, congregations have diminished as people move to the suburbs, so collections at services are likely to be small.

It should be noted that many of these churches still hold regular Sunday services and often weekday services or special musical events as well. If you are intrigued by a particular church on this walk, check to see what services are offered and make a point of attending. Visitors are always made welcome and some churches even provide coffee after a service, which gives you a chance to meet people. And the atmosphere changes when a church is being put to its original use, rather than being merely appreciated for its architecture.

We begin at St Mary-le-Bow, a church that traditionally defines the centre of the City of London. To be born within the sound of the Bow bells was to make the child a true Londoner, a 'cockney'. Today, of course, few people can claim that distinction, for most of the City is no longer residential. But for us it will be an appropriate place to begin.

St Mary-le-Bow is in Cheapside, on the corner of Bow Lane, a very short distance west from the St Paul's Underground station, almost equally close to Mansion House Underground, which is just down Bow Lane. In addition, a number of buses go past the church, for Cheapside is part of the long east–west path through London that starts with Bayswater Road just north of Hyde Park, then becomes Oxford Street, High Holborn, Holborn Viaduct and Newgate Street. After Cheapside, it becomes Poultry, which leads to the great financial centre of the City that we visited on the introductory walk.

There has been a church on this site at least since the eleventh century and perhaps earlier; parts of the much older Norman structure can be seen in the present crypt, including a number of Norman round arches, or 'bows',

116

which give the church its name. But Wren's great contribution here is the tower and steeple, thought by many to be his finest achievement. Luckily the tower and steeple were not damaged in 1941, although the inside of the church was destroyed.

The interior is large and grand, as befits a church built in the centre of commerce (the 'Chepe' that gives a name to Cheapside was originally a market-place and many of the adjoining streets like 'Poultry' or 'Bread' or 'Wood' explain which merchants did business there), but it is largely modern, with some fine stained glass and a unique carved wooden cross given to the church after the last war by the people of Germany. The interior lacks the fine detail and intimate feeling of a Wren church; it is likely that his only contribution was the magnificent tower, surmounted by a huge golden dragon and containing the famous Bow bells. Some might be interested to note that the psalm inscriptions on the twelve bells form an acrostic — the first letters of each inscription spell 'D. Whittington', for Dick Whittington, the almost legendary Lord Mayor of London.

We walk now to St Mary Aldermary, which faces Queen Victoria Street, just down Bow Lane across from the Mansion House Underground station. This church undoubtedly dates back a long time, for the name 'Aldermary' means 'the older Mary' — older, that is, than the other St Mary churches in the City. Some of that remote past can be seen in ancient remnants of older walls, some in the medieval style of its decoration. The interior was designed by Wren and it is one of his few experiments with the Gothic style, occasioned by the request of one of its benefactors after the Great Fire that the church be rebuilt as it had been before.

The most striking medieval feature of the church is the fan vaulting on the roof, which probably echoes the original ceiling that Wren was trying to copy. He also made the tower medieval; it is strikingly different from his others.

We'll walk next down towards the river to see 'Wren's Lantern', crossing the busy Mansion House intersection and moving south down Garlick Hill. St James, Garlickhythe, perhaps named because garlic was once sold on the river's edge below, is in some ways a typical Wren church. Called 'Wren's Lantern' because of the brilliance of light inside from the round-headed and clerestory windows, replaced with clear glass after the bombing of 1941, it has the tallest City church interior and has been carefully restored since the war. There are many details of carving and ironwork that are worth close examination; the three-tiered steeple is a variation on one of Wren's favourite styles. We'll see some of the others later.

As we move on to St Michael Paternoster Royal, the next church on our walk, you should note that the area through which you are walking offers many interesting sights, both old and new. Every year new warehouses and office buildings appear here, but in between are some of the old guild halls. And always, of course, there are glimpses of the river between warehouses and docks.

The best way to approach the next church is to walk down Garlick Hill to Upper Thames Street, turn left past College Hill and then left again up Dowgate Hill. At some point on Dowgate Hill, soon after you pass College Street on your left, you should be able to see the two steeples of St James, Garlickhythe, and St Michael Paternoster Royal against the sky, just as Wren intended. They provide fascinating variations on the same theme: the one with its three diminishing squares and square ornamentation at the corners, the other with its round colonnades, round urns for decoration and a round turret. Such contrasts were often in Wren's mind when he designed his towers and steeples, but his intentions have often been thwarted now by the intervention of new large buildings that cut off the view.

To get to the church it will be necessary to walk west over College Street. St Michael Paternoster Royal was almost completely gutted in the war; only the tower and walls remained. But it has been rebuilt and the open area now facing the river has been retained, as Dick Whittington Gardens; it has pleasant landscaping and benches where the walker can take a brief rest.

This is Dick Whittington's church. The famous citizen and four times Lord Mayor in the late fourteenth and early fifteenth century lived just up the street and is buried here, although his tomb was destroyed, along with the entire church, in the fire of 1666. Whittington gave large sums of money to the building and maintenance of the old church and his name will always be associated with it.

Wren rebuilt it after the Great Fire and it was rebuilt again after war bombing. Inside there is much to be seen: a splendid carved wooden pulpit attributed to Grinling Gibbons, the famous seventeenth-century carver, much original ironwork and a fine seventeenth-century candelabra taken from all Hallows the Great, a nearby church that was not rebuilt after the Second World War.

We'll have a short walk in the fresh air to the next church, St Stephen Walbrook. Retrace your steps along College Street to Dowgate Hill, go up the hill and across busy Cannon Street you will find Walbrook. On the right, just before you get to Mansion House, is the church.

The steeple is interesting — another variation on the diminishing square porches, this time diminishing almost to a point. It is hard to see between buildings, but if you look closely you may also be able to see the green copper exterior of the dome, which is St Stephen Walbrook's most distinguishing feature.

Wren designed this dome before he built St Paul's Cathedral; you should be able to see some similarities between this small version and the greater conception embodied in the cathedral. The dome and the sixteen large columns that divide the interior space make this one of Wren's most interesting churches. Unfortunately for the visitor, the church has been closed in recent years while renovation work goes on. It is not clear when it will again be open to the public, but you should at least make the attempt, for the interior is well worth seeing.

Our next church is St Mary Woolnoth, not far away, but it will require a little ingenuity to get there. The easy way is to continue up Walbrook to the Mansion House intersection and then go right into Lombard Street; the adventuresome might wish to turn right on the little street just beyond St Stephen Walbrook and work through the maze of little lanes to King William Street.

St Mary Woolnoth fills the narrow space between King

William and Lombard Streets. It is one of only two churches on this walk that was not created by Christopher Wren; it was designed by his pupil Hawksmoor. It therefore offers an interesting contrast to Wren's work.

Clearly Hawksmoor shares Wren's love of light and decoration, but he is more mathematically minded, more concerned with regularity and balance; hence the effect is somewhat heavier, more solid. You will no doubt find other comparisons between pupil and master. It is also worth noting that his may be the only church in the world with an Underground station in its basement.

To get to the next church you should continue down King William Street until you come to Abchurch Lane, which leads to St Mary Abchurch. Alternatively you can go down Sherborne Lane, which will give you the best view of the tower and steeple.

The interior, however, is the most interesting part of St Mary Abchurch. Wren was here again experimenting with domes, and this small but handsome dome is painted. Although the interior was damaged in 1940, the painting is the restored original. Also worth noting is the marvellous carved woodwork, including an authentic Grinling Gibbons reredos (the ornamental screen behind the altar); Gibbons's receipt for the work still exists in the parish records.

Many people feel that St Mary Abchurch is one of Wren's most beautiful churches, and we are fortunate that much of the interior is the same as it was in the eighteenth century. The church will repay close study from different positions to see the play of light and shadow on the dark wood pews, light coloured walls and the painted ceiling.

Our next short walk will take us past another one of Wren's constructions — the Monument to the Great Fire of 1666. Walk west on Cannon Street to the major intersection where a road to the right leads across London Bridge, continue west a few steps to Fish Street Hill, turn right a few steps and the monument will be in front of you.

Since this is an area of new high-rise office buildings, it is difficult to think back on the time when the monument towered over its surroundings — now hundreds of people in

MONUMENT TO THE GREAT FIRE OF LONDON

offices look down on the top of it. When it was finished in 1671, it was one of the highest points in the City; when James Boswell climbed to the top years later, he reported in his journal that he felt giddy from the height and had the impression that he could see all of London.

It is still possible to climb to the observation platform at the top, if you can manage the 311 steps, but your view will be somewhat limited by the tall buildings all around you. The column is 202 feet high, and its base is supposedly exactly 202 feet from the point the Great Fire started, in Pudding Lane, to the east.

But this is a walk to look at churches, so we now proceed on down Fish Street Hill and across Lower Thames Street to St Magnus the Martyr. Indeed, the church itself has become a martyr to surrounding warehouses and office buildings, so that it is difficult to see, let alone enter. But the struggle is worth the effort, for both interior and exterior are rewarding.

The stone tower and domed lantern were intended as a welcome to people coming across the old London Bridge; the walkway from the bridge actually went under the tower and directly past the entrance to the church. Inside you can still find unexpected splendour, white and gold brilliantly lit by clear glass clerestory windows, a beautifully proportioned barrel-vaulted ceiling. Perhaps the most unexpected thing is that this church should still be standing on this valuable commercial property.

We now go back up the hill, away from the river for the last time on this walk, to find St Mary-at-Hill. We walk west along Lower Thames Street, past the old Billingsgate Fish Market on the right, now closed, although some of the smells may remain, until we come to a street called St Mary-at-Hill.

Halfway up this short street you will see a clock projecting above the pavement; this is the east wall of St Mary-at-Hill, but getting into the church is not so easy. Just beyond the clock is a small walkway that will lead to a churchyard but not to the entrance; to get in you must find Lovat Lane, which runs past the west tower.

Once inside, you will find a different world, one which should be familiar by now. St Mary-at-Hill provides a richness that shocks because of the contrast with the narrow lanes and plain brick walls outside; here is another sample of the care taken by parishioners and public to hold back the commercial tide from these small areas of calm and beauty.

Very little needs to be said about this interior. If you have come this far on this walk you will have seen enough to make your own comparisons. Make sure you note the marvellous pulpit, with its long carved wooden staircase.

From your earlier position beneath the clock of St Mary-at-Hill you could have looked up the hill to see the steeple of St Margaret Pattens. Unlike St Mary-at-Hill, St Margaret Pattens can be seen from various angles in the area, but like all these City churches it is closely surrounded by modern buildings. St Margaret Pattens is the last Wren church we shall visit on this walk. It is worth noting that the name may come from the wooden 'pattens' or clogs that people once wore to keep their feet out of the muddy streets. They may have been manufactured in this district.

Now we shall take a brief walk past the ruin of another Wren church, St Dunstan-in-the-East, on our way to All-Hallows-by-the-Tower, the last church we shall visit today. After St Margaret Pattens, continue west along Great Tower Street for just a few steps until you find the narrow Idol Lane to the left. The tower and some walls of St Dunstan-in-the-East remain from the bombings of the last war. The interior has not been restored, but has instead been planted with grass and flowers and made into a delightful little park and place of rest. You may wish to sit on a bench for a few moments, resting your feet and imagining what this Wren church might have looked like in the late seventeenth century when it was first built.

From here it is just a short distance to All-Hallows-by-the-Tower. Continue down Great Tower Street until you see the church in front of you. This is a church that survived the Great Fire of 1666; in fact, Samuel Pepys, the diarist, climbed its tower to get a view of the fire. But what the fire of 1666 could not do, the bombing of 1940 did: the church was destroyed and has since been rebuilt.

All-Hallows-by-the-Tower is rich in history and makes an appropriate place to end this walk, for it stands by the Tower of London, the eastern gateway to the old City of London, and surveys the area we have explored. This church, more than many we have seen, welcomes visitors; inside you will find an abundance of printed materials explaining the history of the church, and there are often knowledgeable guides on hand who will be happy to provide more information.

Having seen a dozen or so of these fine City churches, you should remember that there are dozens more for your inspection. Not only in the City, of course, but in other areas

ST PAUL'S CATHEDRAL

of London. And at some time every visitor to London must spend time in Wren's masterpiece, St Paul's Cathedral, near where this walk began. Perhaps if you postpone your visit to St Paul's until after you have examined a number of Wren's earlier designs, you will be better equipped to appreciate the breathtaking magnificence of his greatest creation, and also appreciate the epitaph which he wrote for his tomb in the north transept of St Paul's: 'If you would see his monument, look around you.'

The Thames
and Greenwich

'I should counsel you to remove your court
to Greenwich and convert St James's Palace
into a hospital.'

Peter the Great to King William

WHEN THE Russian ruler gave this advice to William and
Mary in the late seventeenth century he was marvelling at
the beauty of the area we will visit today; we can only be
grateful that William did not take his advice, for if
Greenwich were the official residence it would not be open
to the public.

But Greenwich has always belonged to the monarchy,
even though in the public mind the place is associated with
an observatory, the location of the zero degree meridian,
the place that established the time of day. Greenwich Mean
Time (GMT) has been a standard throughout the world
since the late nineteenth century, when most of the nations
agreed to its adoption, but the Greenwich standard had
been used long before that by sailors — in fact it was to
improve navigation that Charles II established the
observatory, not from any idle curiosity about the heavens.

Henry VIII was the first monarch to live at Greenwich, at
least part of the time. He was in fact born here and baptized
in the church of St Alfege — still standing and available for
a visit. Henry lived here with his first queen, Katherine, and
it was here he began his relationship with Anne Boleyn that
finally led to his breaking away from the Church of Rome.

OLD PALACE AT GREENWICH

The Queen's House, a beautiful small villa that is now the centrepiece of the National Maritime Museum, was built later for Queen Anne of Denmark, the wife of James I. The architect was Inigo Jones, and the residence is another early example of the Palladian style that Jones had brought from Italy.

Charles I finally completed the Queen's House for his bride, Henrietta Maria, and they spent a long-delayed honeymoon in what they called their 'house of delight'. But Charles was executed, and Greenwich was neglected until his son regained the throne in 1660. Charles II added to the villa and tore down some of the other buildings in the area to open a view to the river. He also began some of the other buildings that now provide such a spectacular view from the Thames. He laid out Greenwich Park on the other side of the villa and established the first observatory on the hill, in a building designed by Christopher Wren in 1675. It must have been a very interesting task for Wren since he had started his own career as an astronomer.

It was Charles's niece, Mary, with her husband William of Orange who, perhaps regretfully, ignored Peter the Great's advice and hired Christopher Wren to design further buildings in the area, not for a palace, but as a hospital for retired and disabled sailors, in honour of Charles II and to provide a naval counterpart for his hospital for army veterans at Chelsea (see Walk No. 18). The hospital was later moved and the buildings became the Royal Naval College for the advanced education of naval officers.

We should now consider the matter of getting there, which in this case is half the fun. Greenwich can be reached by train or bus, but the river is by far the most pleasant route. Perhaps the best plan is to take a boat downstream and return by bus. Be sure to bring a woollen jumper or jacket; it's always colder on the river than on shore. And you might like to carry a camera, because there will be spectacular views; if you have binoculars, bring those along too.

ROYAL HOSPITAL, GREENWICH

127

Boats leave regularly during the summer from Westminster Pier, where we took our first ride on the Thames in Walk No. 1. You can ride in comfort to Greenwich in about forty-five minutes, but perhaps an even more interesting approach is to take a boat not to Greenwich but beyond, to the very new Thames Barrier, which will take about an hour and a quarter. This way you also get the best views of the Naval College and the Queen's House from the river; the four buildings of the college are arranged in a square, with the two furthest from the river a little closer together, so that you get an exaggerated sense of perspective, as between them, and behind, you see the charming small Queen's House. Up the hill, in the distance, stands the old observatory.

In a few minutes, around the bend of the river, the Thames Barrier will appear, like a scaly monster heaving out of the water. Actually, the barrier is a modern engineering marvel designed to control the tides. The Thames, of course, is a tidal river, all the way to London and further upstream — massive tides at that, sometimes more than twenty feet. Before the embankment was constructed, much of the area just north of the river was subject to flooding with depressing regularity. After the embankment was built the danger of floods decreased, but there have been several occasions in recent years when the river overflowed, causing much damage.

Thus the Thames Barrier was erected, a series of massive movable gates a few miles downstream from Greenwich, where the river is one-third of a mile across. At the threat of a flood tide, ten huge gates mounted between gigantic stainless steel piers swing up and block the water. At other times, shipping — even large vessels — slips easily through the openings, while the gates rest below in concrete pillows on the riverbed.

The stainless steel pylons that contain the operating mechanism for the gates rise five storeys from the water and make a sight almost as memorable as the Gothic pillars of Tower Bridge. The trip is well worth the detour, particularly because the builders of the barrier have also installed pleasant gardens along the bank for visitors, with a café, a souvenir shop and a narrated sound and slide show that gives a brief but fascinating discussion of the Thames and the building of the barrier.

When you want to go back to Greenwich you have two choices: there are boats that make the trip up river in about twenty-five minutes, but there is a much quicker bus every half hour or so that takes only five minutes, perhaps a little longer in Sunday traffic. You'll see the reason for the length of the boat trip if you look at a map; the Thames makes a tremendous bend at this point, while the road goes direct.

The bus from the barrier will drop you at Greenwich in Romney Road, between the Royal Naval College and the Queen's House, which — along with its two newer wings — houses the Maritime Museum. Here you are in the middle of Greenwich's various attractions.

If you have not yet had lunch, there are many possibilities. Straight ahead is the centre of Greenwich, which has a number of restaurants and pubs. The museum has a lunch room as well. Perhaps the most famous pub in Greenwich, the Trafalgar Tavern, is on Park Row, at the river's edge, not far east of the college. The rooms are named after Nelson's admirals and some of them have fine views. There are inexpensive bar snacks as well as a somewhat more elaborate restaurant.

But we'll begin our exploration of Greenwich with the Maritime Museum. The museum is arranged chronologically: seventeenth-century items and earlier are in the Queen's House, exhibits up to 1815 are kept in the west wings and more modern materials can be found in the smaller east wing. The Queen's House interior has a good deal of architectural interest; the entry hall is a perfect cube, splendidly decorated, with a ceiling painted by Thornhill, Hogarth's father-in-law. And there is a fine circular staircase.

As for the maritime exhibits, they present a multitude of riches, more than the spectator can appreciate in one visit. Included are portraits of naval heroes and paintings of naval battles, some by famous painters. There are marvellously intricate ship models, some of them twenty feet long. Whole rooms are devoted to Captain Cook and to Admiral

Nelson. And in the New Neptune Hall you can see and walk on a number of actual historic vessels, one of which is so large it seems as irreconcilable as a ship in a bottle. The Barge House adjacent has a wonderfully decorated state barge built by William Kent in 1732 for Frederick, Prince of Wales. Crimson and gilt, it looks like a royal coach dropped on a long narrow hull, with room for twenty-two rowers, two french horns and about six passengers.

If you are fascinated by the history of man's conquest of the sea, the Maritime Museum will take a lot of your time and attention, but now we will walk up the hill, across Greenwich Park, to the old Royal Observatory. The new observatory is located out of London, where the air is clearer; this one is now an extension of the museum, with many of the original observatory instruments and a great collection of clocks and chronometers.

It is probably less than a quarter of a mile walk up the hill and from the top you will get a fine view in every direction. Outside the building, too, is a brass marker identifying the zero meridian — a place where tourists always stop and take each other's pictures astride the marker. Also outside, on a small tower, is the great orange ball that drops precisely at 1 p.m. each afternoon, so that all the ships in the river and at dock can set their chronometers. In fact, their chronometers are now set by radio signals, but the orange ball is still hauled to the top of its staff at 12.55 each day, and dropped exactly on the hour.

The walking tour through the buildings begins at the oldest, Flamsteed House, named after the first Astronomer Royal, for whom it was built. Originally both residence and observatory, the octagonal room, with its old-fashioned telescopes peering out of the windows, is the most fascinating. One of the Flamsteed's clocks is still operating, with a pendulum so long that its face is upstairs while the pendulum rocks back and forth a storey below.

From here, arrows will lead you from room to room, and from this building to the newer observatory, through a seemingly endless collection of instruments for observing the sky and keeping time. If you are interested, in the souvenir shop at the end of the walk you can buy a kit to make your own cardboard astrolabe or backstaff.

There is much of Greenwich Park still to explore, if you feel like a walk in the country, and to the south lies Blackheath, which used to be a place where highwaymen waylaid their victims but now offers a good area for a family picnic. Eventually, however, you'll have to go down the hill again into Greenwich to take a look at the other things worth visiting.

King William Walk will lead you back down through the town and to the pier, if you want to take a boat up river. To the right is the Royal Naval College, where you may walk through part of the grounds and visit two buildings, but only after 2.30 in the afternoon. The chapel was rebuilt in the late eighteenth century and contains statues and an altarpiece by Benjamin West. The Painted Hall across the way is one of the world's most elaborate dining-rooms, with a marvellous ceiling by Sir James Thornhill; his *trompe l'oeil* painting loops down over the walls creating a most intriguing illusion.

To the left from King William Walk, along Romney Road, stands the church of St Alfege. And finally, at the waterfront, near the pier, are two vastly different but immensely interesting ships in dry dock. The *Cutty Sark* is one of the last of the great nineteenth-century sailing clippers, in a permanent concrete dry dock, where you can examine it inside and out. Inside there is a collection of figureheads and other objects of interest.

Near the *Cutty Sark* stands the *Gipsy Moth IV*, the very small yacht in which Sir Francis Chichester sailed alone around the world in 1968. If the *Cutty Sark* impresses the visitor by its great size, *Gipsy Moth* will surely impress with its smallness. Perhaps she seemed snug to her captain, but to most of us she looks distinctly claustrophobic.

There is also a pedestrian tunnel underneath the Thames at this point, leading to the Isle of Dogs. The entrance is near *Gypsy Moth IV*.

Now that the time has come to head back to London, the boat is right at hand. The trip back will probably take a little longer, because you will be going upstream. Perhaps a more interesting trip, if you have already taken the boat one way,

131

is the bus, which will lead you through a variety of London suburbs on the way back. You'll want the No. 188, which leaves from King William Walk, next to the Royal Naval College. Be sure to take a bus going away from the river. Since this is the beginning of the route, you should be able to get a good seat upstairs, perhaps even the front one, which will give the best view.

Your route will take you through Rotherhithe, Bermondsey, past the famous junction called Elephant and Castle, past Waterloo Station and over Waterloo Bridge into central London. From there the bus goes up Kingsway to Holborn and then on to King's Cross. If you consult your map, you will find one of those junctions convenient for the rest of your journey.

Marylebone

Through Manchester Square took a canter just now —
  Met the *old yellow chariot*, and make a low bow.
This I did, of course, thinking 'twas loyal and civil
  But got such a look, oh, 'twas black as the devil!
How unlucky! — incog: he was travelling about,
  And I, like a noodle, must go find him out!
Mem: when next by the *old yellow chariot* I ride
  To remember there *is* nothing princely inside.

Tom Moore

PRONOUNCE IT any way you like, everybody does; in his
diary, Pepys wrote it as 'Marrow-bone', but he was
probably thinking of his dinner. Marylebone was a village a
mile or so from central London in the seventeenth century
and earlier; in the eighteenth century it became a
fashionable suburb. The name is derived from a river and
church: the river Tyburn (which also gave its name to a
nearby gallows) used to flow south to the Thames but is now
underground; the village church was St Mary-a-le-bourne
(beside the stream). After the inevitable elision it became
Marylebone.

We are once more in the fashionable West End — west,
that is, of the City. Henry VIII had a hunting park in this
area, but it wasn't until the eighteenth century when
wealthy families began to move to the suburbs that the
village of Marylebone came alive.

As in other places, the rich built elaborate houses around
open squares — we'll look at three of them today — and in
the late eighteenth century the then Prince of Wales

133

('Prinny' to the people), who was to become George IV late in his life, persuaded his favourite architect, John Nash, to develop Regent Street as a main thoroughfare from the public buildings of Whitehall towards the countrified area that later grew into Regent's Park. Of course that accelerated the population move westward and northward.

We'll begin this walk at Portman Square, a little north-east of Marble Arch. Marble Arch is easily reachable by Underground or bus; from there it's just a short walk down Oxford Street to Portman Street and then left.

Portman Square is now surrounded mostly by office blocks and hotels, but on the north side, at No. 20, is Home House, former residence of the Countess of Home and one of Robert Adam's finest surviving town houses. Home House now belongs to the Courtauld Institute of Art of the University of London, which operates the Witt Library of European paintings and drawings next door. The house itself is usually open to the public, as is the Heinz Gallery next door, which maintains an exhibit of architects' drawings.

Besides Mrs Home, another famous widow lived in Portman Square in the eighteenth century. Mrs Elizabeth Montagu, one of the educated 'blue-stockings', was Mrs Home's rival in entertaining distinguished visitors, and it would seem that Mrs Montagu won hands down. Her guests included such luminaries as Samuel Johnson, Fanny Burney, Mr and Mrs Thrale and Horace Walpole. Her house has disappeared to the developers, but perhaps you can close your eyes and ears to the traffic and imagine what it would have been like to roll up in your carriage to meet Dr Johnson, to drink a dish of chocolate with Horace Walpole, and to discuss the issues of the day.

On the east side of Portman Square is Baker Street, a familiar name to all fans of Sherlock Holmes; the great detective had rooms at '221B' Baker Street, which should be north of Marylebone Road, but you won't find it if you look. Still, someone up there apparently answers mail that is regularly sent to Conan Doyle's fictional character.

Baker Street is a rather ordinary shopping street so we'll cross it quickly and head east from Portman Square along

Harding Street, to find ourselves almost at once in Manchester Square. Here we'll find Hertford House, the home of the Wallace Collection, where we should stop for a while.

Hertford House is a lovely eighteenth-century family mansion—one of the few left around the square. The gossip about one of the ladies Hertford and 'Prinny' gave rise to Tom Moore's little poem that opens this walk. The Prince of Wales drove a very distinctive yellow coach, one that was immediately recognizable, and he did not hesitate to park it most of the night outside Hertford House during the time he was madly infatuated with Lady Hertford.

And, of course, during that period he was married to the cantankerous Queen Caroline, who tried to crash his coronation (see Walk No. 19). Prinny was a favourite of Londoners, in spite of — or perhaps because of — his indiscretions, but everyone had to laugh at this affair, since both parties were well into middle age and — to be blunt — grossly fat. There was even a satiric print of the couple widely circulated in the eighteenth century — hard to find now — called *Manchester Fair Cattle Show*.

Years later, the house passed to the natural son of the fourth Marquess of Hertford, Sir Richard Wallace, whose wife bequeathed the family collections to the nation at the end of the nineteenth century. The Wallace Collection contains some of the finest paintings and art objects in London; you will be amazed at how much is packed into a relatively small house. In addition, the house itself is a treasure and the exhibits are arranged with great taste — furniture, porcelain and ornaments match the paintings that hang in each room. You may wish to spend quite a bit of time here.

The Wallace Collection is particularly rich in European painting. One room, for example, contains important works by Watteau, Lancret, Boucher and Fragonard. Other rooms display earlier art, with works by Hans Holbein the Younger, Rembrandt, Van Dyck, Titian and Rubens. There is a fascinating collection of old clocks, several in every room, and an important collection of arms and armour.

It is possible that the Wallace Collection may capture your attention for the rest of the day. If so, this is an easy place to end the walk — Oxford Street, and Selfridges department store, are just south, and Bond Street Underground station is a short distance east along Oxford Street.

But if you wish to continue, we'll walk a little further east to one more residential square before we turn north towards Marylebone Road. Leave Manchester Square to the south and turn left at Wigmore Street, which is full of fashionable shops. You will also find a few small restaurants along here and on some of the nearby streets — good places to stop if it is lunch-time.

Soon Wigmore Street will lead you into the north side of Cavendish Square, the oldest and perhaps the brightest of the eighteenth-century residential squares. You will see a number of houses around the square with architectural details that will seem familiar by this time. There is no particular house to visit, but many well-known people lived here in the past.

Lady Mary Wortley Montagu was one. An older cousin of the Portman Square Montagus, she was a great hostess, a clever letter writer and a witty conversationalist; one of her claims to fame is that the brilliant but rather ugly and misshapen poet, Alexander Pope, once declared his love for her and she laughed in his face. A dangerous thing to do — he never forgave her and lampooned her viciously in some of his later verse.

Lady Mary had an interesting relationship with Lord Hervey, a man of what the eighteenth century called 'indeterminate sex' — Pope called him 'a gilded bug' who 'stinks and stings'. Lady Mary, who was supposed to be Hervey's friend, is on record as saying that human beings were divided into three sexes, men, women and Herveys. Much later in her life, Hervey got his revenge. Lady Mary became infatuated with a young Italian. She followed him to Italy, only to discover that she had lost him to a rival — Lord Hervey.

Another resident of Cavendish Square — before he went bankrupt — was Richard Brinsley Sheridan, the playwright and manager for a while of the Theatre Royal in Drury Lane (see Walk No. 12). He was the author of some of the most popular comedies in the late eighteenth century — *The Rivals* and *The School for Scandal* — but he was also an inveterate gambler, playboy and friend of the profligate 'Prinny', who led him into escapades and debt.

Sheridan had been married — in the Marylebone parish church that we'll pass at the end of this walk — to one of the most beautiful women of his time, Elizabeth Linley. Sheridan could never be faithful to her, much as he loved her, but when she died very young he was devastated. It was all downhill after that; his second marriage, to a very young girl, failed; and he was finally arrested for debt. But during the good years, when he was a wealthy Member of Parliament, a member of Johnson's Literary Club and a friend of royalty, he helped to make Cavendish Square glitter.

Harley Street, traditionally the street of physicians, especially expensive ones, runs north from Cavendish Square, but we'll go east a little further and head north along Regent Street and Portland Place. At the top of Regent Street, visible all the way from Oxford Circus, is All Souls' Church, designed by Nash in 1823 to make an emphatic conclusion to the broad avenue that he had designed. There is a bust of the architect in the portico of the church, and its round, needle-like spire is a London landmark.

After the curve to the left of Langham Place, around All Souls', we get to Portland Place, with the huge Broadcasting House, the headquarters of the BBC, on the right. Portland Place was once another avenue of stately and expensive town houses, a number of them built by the Adam brothers, but many are now giving way to public buildings of various kinds.

With all this luxury and splendour, you may think that only the rich could walk these streets. But the Wesley brothers, Charles and John, also lived in Marylebone and they often joined the fashionable crowds to watch the hangings at Tyburn — not for entertainment, but to provide religious consolation to the poor wretches who climbed the

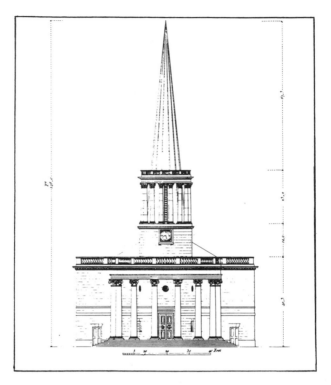

ALL SOULS CHURCH, LANGHAM PLACE

scaffold. The Wesley brothers were the founders of
Methodism, an eighteenth-century reform movement
within the English Church, and Charles was the author of
many hymns that are still sung in churches today, including
'Hark, the Herald Angels Sing' and 'Jesu, Lover of My
Soul'.

The Wesley brothers could not have approved of all the
social activity that dominated Marylebone, especially the
prostitutes who followed the wealthy and who at one time
constituted a substantial part of Marylebone's population,
mostly east of Portland Place. According to one estimate,

there may have been as many as 13,000 living here at the end of the eighteenth century, including one who became particularly famous — partly because of what she charged (100 guineas a night) and partly because she was a favourite model of Sir Joshua Reynolds. Her name was Kitty Fisher and she came to a sad end, of which the moralists might approve, dying at the age of twenty-six.

At the northern end of Portland Place is Park Crescent, a splendid semi-circle of stately town houses also built by Nash. The semi-circular pattern was a favourite of Nash and other planners of his time; if you travel to Bath you will see the same idea carried to an even grander conclusion (see Walk No. 22).

On the other side of Park Crescent lies Regent's Park, but that's for another day's exploration (see Walk No. 16). For now, if you have walked enough, there are two Underground stations here, one right in the middle of Park Crescent, the other, Great Portland Street station, a short distance to the east. There are also a number of buses along Marylebone Road. We will conclude this walk with a few words about Marylebone Road itself.

Marylebone Road is a very busy street, with heavy traffic; it is not much fun to walk along. But a little less than a quarter of a mile west, on the left side of the road, Marylebone High Street curves off to the south, following the village path of 200 years ago. This junction is the site of the old village church we mentioned at the beginning of this walk. The church is gone, but the area is now a garden of rest. You can find the graves of Charles and John Wesley here, as well as the architect James Gibbs and the painters Allan Ramsay and George Stubbs. It is perhaps a restful place to sit and relax before hurrying home.

Across Marylebone Road is the London Planetarium and Madame Tussaud's Waxworks, which has lifelike representations of historical figures and tableaux. A little further along is the Baker Street Underground, and Baker Street, which has one-way traffic going south, carries a number of buses that will take you back to the central city.

Regent's Park, the Zoo

Jackal, jackal, loudly bark,
In the zoo at Regent's Park.
What immortal eye or hand
Put you so close to my bit of land?

Anon

THIS WALK picks up where the last one left off, at the top of Portland Place, in Park Crescent, the southern edge of Regent's Park. It is another walk for a sunny day, although the park has its own charm on those misty, drizzly days that are typical of London weather — if you are brave enough to face the elements.

With its 470 acres, Regent's Park is smaller than Hyde Park and Kensington Gardens, but it is much more beautifully landscaped, and the variety of waterfowl that inhabit its artificial lake rivals that of St James's Park. In June, the roses in Queen Mary's Garden, the circular centre of the park, are truly spectacular.

Regent's Park was not really intended as a public park. Originally, it included more of Henry VIII's hunting area, but in the early nineteenth century, when the then Prince Regent commissioned Nash to design the park, the Regent thought of it as a large residential area, for himself and for others who could afford a country villa this close to London.

Those dreams never materialized, although some of the residences in Park Crescent to the south and in some of the terraces on the eastern border reflect the intended residential nature of the area. But the pressures of commercial development proved too strong to resist, and Regent's Park became a place for public strolling and picnics, rather than a private parkland for the few who could afford to live here.

You can get to Park Crescent, where we'll begin this walk, by taking a bus up Marylebone Road or Portland Street, or by travelling by Underground to the Regent's Park or Great Portland Street station. From Park Crescent, cross Marylebone Road at either the west or east end, walk up Park Square and you will find yourself at the Outer Circle, a road that goes around the outer perimeter of the park.

As you can see by looking at your map, Regent's Park has a variety of pathways for walkers; you may choose any of them that suit your inclination and energy. We'll suggest one walk that ends at the zoo, with some other possibilities along the way.

First, turn west along the Outer Circle and look at the symmetrical buildings on your left, on York Terrace — remnants of the original plan for the park. To the right very soon you will begin to get glimpses of the lake, and at York Gate you may turn right, cross the bridge over the lake and proceed northward to the Inner Circle which, in beautifully regular geometry, defines the inner gardens, Queen Mary's.

These small gardens may be the most beautifully landscaped in all of London; a leisurely stroll through this area is highly recommended. And you should note, in the north-west area, the open-air theatre where Shakespeare performances are put on during the summer, sometimes modified but rarely cancelled by the weather.

When you are ready to leave Queen Mary's Gardens, walk along Chester Road to the east, until you come to Broad Walk, and then turn north again. Broad Walk is a magnificent tree-lined path that will lead you direct to the zoo if you wish, or to numerous other branching roads if you want to prolong your stay in the park. One of those roads, to the north-west, will take you to Winfield House, built by the American heiress Barbara Hutton in 1936 and now the residence of the American ambassador.

GIRAFFE HOUSE

But if you continue along the Broad Walk, there are
splendid terrace dwellings that can be seen just beyond the
Outer Circle. This is a marvellous place to live, particularly
since you may be awakened by the distant roar of a lion, or,
if the wind is right, even the smell of the lion's den.

The London Zoo, more properly the Gardens of the
Zoological Society of London, was established here almost
as soon as the park itself was laid out in the early nineteenth
century, but the zoo has undergone many changes and
modifications since then. There seems little reason to
describe the zoo at any length. If you like zoos, and visit
them whenever you can, you know what to expect; if you
don't care for zoos, there are plenty of paths in the park that
will take you another direction.

The South Gate to the zoo is just off the Broad Walk and
there are excellent publications to describe the exhibits
inside. You can easily spend a half day or more here; we'll

discuss a brief continuation of this walk if you skip the zoo or take merely a short visit, and we'll mention the quickest way home if you decide to spend the rest of your day inside.

First, then, for an immediate return from the zoo. Leave by the North Gate, which will deposit you on Prince Albert Road. There you should look for the No. 74 bus going west, or left, which will take you down Park Road, to the west of the park, Baker Street to Oxford Street, Marble Arch, south to Hyde Park Corner and then west down Cromwell Road. If it is a Sunday in summer, you may also catch a No. 2 bus at this point, which follows the 74 as far as Hyde Park Corner, but then goes south to its terminus at Victoria Station.

If you have time and would like a pleasant and more leisurely departure from the zoo, catch one of the long, narrow canal boats on the Regent's Canal, which runs through the northern end of the zoo. The canal bus will take you through St John's Wood, a pleasant residential area once much favoured by artists and bohemians, through a short tunnel, and finally to Little Venice, a broadening of the canal where there are many gaily painted boats and well-maintained Victorian houses. The area was named by the poet Robert Browning.

At Little Venice you are not far from the Warwick Avenue Underground station (on the Bakerloo line), and not far west from Edgware Road, which has many buses going south to Marble Arch.

It is also possible to do this walk from back to front, particularly if your chief interest is the zoo. You can catch regular shuttle boats near Little Venice that will take you directly to the zoo and the price of the trip will include your fees for entrance to the zoo. Or, in the summer, you can take a longer trip through the zoo all the way to Camden Town, a pleasant suburb to the north of Regent's Park, with a good shopping area and lots of restaurants. Finally, you can find canal boats at Little Venice that specialize in luncheon or dinner cruises, who will serve you a meal while you glide along the narrow waterways.

Hampstead

To one who has been long in city pent,
'Tis very sweet to look into the fair
And open face of heaven.

Keats

KEATS CHOSE Hampstead as a place to live because, for him
and many others, it provided the 'face of heaven' after the
bustle and grime of the city. Surprisingly, Hampstead is still
an attractive, village-like suburb, a place where the ground
rises into hills, where the air seems to be cleaner and where
London is only a pleasant misty view in the distance.

Hampstead is rich in charm and history; besides the poet
Keats (who lived here for only two very productive years),
two important painters, John Constable and George
Romney, lived and worked in this area. You'll see many of
their Hampstead paintings in various galleries, and
Constable is buried in the local cemetery.

Besides this, Hampstead is the site of a huge, still almost
wild parkland, where highwaymen used to roam and
families now picnic, a place where you can get a marvellous
panoramic view of much of London. There are still many
lovely eighteenth-century homes in Hampstead and at least
two outstanding houses that are now museums, Fenton
House, small but very elegant, and Kenwood, so immense
and stately it takes your breath away.

We'll visit all these on this walk, including Keats's house, but it will take a full day. The distances here are much more than in the city and only the most indefatigable walker will plan to do it all on foot. Most of us will be happy to enlist the help of the local bus.

The most convenient way to get to our starting point is by Underground—the Northern line to Hampstead station. A warning: the Northern line splits at Camden Town; from that point there are two legs to the south and two to the north. Any train going north from any central station will take you at least as far as Camden Town, but at that point you must take a train headed for Edgware; the name will appear on an electric sign at the station and on the front of the train itself.

A further warning: if you are using a Central Zone pass, you will need to pay a supplementary fare when you reach Hampstead. You may use the pass to board the train, of course, but when you leave, show your pass to the guard at the gate who will tell you how much more you have to pay. If you return from outside the Central Zone, you will have to pay as you enter.

Hampstead station is right in the heart of the old village, on Hampstead High Street. Begin the walk by turning left as you leave the station, to go up Flask Walk, just around the corner, as far as Well Walk. Both these names tell you that Hampstead was famous years ago for its special well water, which was supposed to cure numerous ills. Along this route you will see many interesting old houses and several excellent secondhand book shops. Keats lived in Well Walk for a short time and so did Constable, the latter at No. 40.

At the corner where Flask Walk becomes Well Walk, turn right at Willow Road and walk to Downshire Hill. Turn right again, then left sharply along Keats Grove and you will soon be at John Keats's house and museum. It is open to visitors every day and contains many interesting memorabilia pertaining to Keats — manuscripts and letters, including some from Keats's friends, early editions of Keats's works and personal items associated with both Keats and Fanny Brawne, who lived with her family in one half of the house. In the front yard stands a plum tree on the spot where Keats wrote 'Ode to a Nightingale'.

From here, go back to Downshire Hill and turn left to Rosslyn Hill, a main thoroughfare. Turn right and walk until you are almost back to the Hampstead Underground station and then find Church Row on your left. Church Row was once Hampstead's most fashionable address; it still contains many handsome eighteenth-century homes.

As you walk along Church Row, look for plaques which tell of famous persons who lived here. Fanny Burney, the novelist, described a ball in this neighbourhood in her novel, *Evelina*. Even earlier, Alexander Pope, the poet, and his friend John Gay, author of *The Beggar's Opera* and *Trivia*, the long poem which provides us with many of the epigraphs for these walks, spent some months here as Gay recuperated from an illness — presumably drinking the waters. Other notables who visited Hampstead were Jonathan Swift, the eighteenth-century satirist, Colley Cibber, actor and theatre manager, and later on Dr Johnson and his circle of friends — the painters Joshua Reynolds and Gainsborough, theatre people like Oliver Goldsmith, David Garrick and Mrs Siddons.

HAMPSTEAD CHURCH

All these people (with the possible exception of Pope, who was a Roman Catholic) would have visited St John's, the parish church of Hampstead, which you will find just a short distance up Church Row. If you want to go inside for a rest, you should also look for the bust of Keats. Outside, in the south-east corner of the tranquil churchyard, near the wall is the altar tomb of John Constable.

Almost across from the church is Holly Walk, which will lead you up the hill to Hampstead Grove, past many fine eighteenth-century houses and to Fenton House. Fenton House was built in 1693; it contains many beautifully furnished rooms with fine exhibits of needlework and porcelain from England, Europe and China. A famous Constable painting of Hampstead Heath is there too, as well as a notable collection of old keyboard instruments — virginals, spinets and a harpsichord used by Handel. Concerts are sometimes given in the music room. But Fenton House is open only a few days each week; if you don't want to be disappointed, call ahead for days and times.

From Fenton House, continue up the hill to Whitestone Pond, where Shelley sailed paper boats to amuse Hampstead children. This is just a short distance from the intersection of North End Road and Spaniards Road, where Jack Straw's Castle stands, an old inn where Dickens used to stay. Nearby also is the stop for the No. 210 bus that will take you north to the next and even more impressive stately home, Kenwood. Some distance along Spaniards Road the bus will squeeze through an old toll stop at the eighteenth-century tavern known as the Spaniards; a mile or so further the bus driver will let you off (be sure to ask) at the drive leading to Kenwood.

Kenwood's principal architect was Robert Adam, who built the central part of the huge mansion in 1767. It later became the property of Lord Iveagh, who gave it to the nation in 1927; hence the place is also called the Iveagh Bequest. Inside, the rooms themselves are impressive, perhaps especially the Adam-designed and decorated library. There is a fine collection of paintings by Bouchet, Pater, Rembrandt, Vermeer, Reynolds, Gainsborough and others.

Outside, the grounds of Kenwood cover 194 acres, but seem larger because they are really a part of Hampstead Heath — it is like having the whole of the heath for your garden. Not far from the house is the tiny thatched building called Dr Johnson's Summerhouse, where the writer used to sit and work or perhaps just relax, when it stood in the garden of the Thrales' house in Streatham. It was moved here in 1968.

Kenwood also includes a restaurant and cafeteria, convenient if you have not yet had lunch. You should note, in planning your walk, that the house is closed on Tuesdays.

A further note: if you want to shorten this walk by

skipping the parish church and Fenton House, you could go directly to Kenwood from Keats's house by catching a No. 268 bus on Rosslyn Hill, at the top of Downshire Hill. This will take you as far as the Whitestone Pond area, where you can catch a No. 210 bus for Kenwood. Ask the driver to show you where to make the change.

Leaving Kenwood, you will need to look for the No. 210 bus again, but you can take it going in either direction. If you go east on Hampstead Lane (continuing the way you came) you should get off at Archway Underground station; if you go west, ask the driver to drop you at Golders Green Underground station. The two stations are on different branches of the Underground, but either will take you back to central London. Some trains, however, will go via Tottenham Court Road and Charing Cross, others will go via Bank.

For the truly ambitious walker, who finds himself or herself leaving Kenwood early in the afternoon on a fine day, it is possible, of course, to walk back down to Hampstead village across the heath, by any one of a number of paths. Such a walk will be at least a mile — even if you don't get lost or take a meandering route — but on a nice summer day you will find yourself just one of many hikers in these lovely hills.

Then let the prudent Walker Shoes provide,
Not of the Spanish or Morocco Hide
The wooden Heel may raise the Dancer's Bound,
And with the 'scallop't Top his Step be crown'd
Let firm, well-hammer'd Soles protect thy Feet
Thro' freezing Snows, and Rains, and soaking Sleet.
Should the big Laste extend the Shoe too wide,
Each Stone will wrench th' unwary Step aside:
And when too short the modish Shoes are worn,
You'll judge the Seasons by your shooting Corn.

John Gay

ALMOST ALL writers about London at some time use the
line, 'London is a collection of villages'. In the eighteenth
century, of course, this was literally true; today, those little
villages have been swallowed up, but the areas where they
existed still seem to retain something of their own quality
and character. This is surely true of the place we will explore
today: a charming village of riverfront residences in the
eighteenth century, parts of it remain the same today.

Chelsea lies along the river south of Hyde Park. If you are
staying somewhere in that area and are a really ambitious
walker (with 'well-hammer'd Soles'), you wouldn't have to
use public transport at all. But most of us would probably
prefer to take the Underground or bus to Sloane Square, for
there will be quite a lot of walking to follow — wear sturdy
shoes, as John Gay suggests. (We hope there will be no
'freezing Snows' or 'soaking Sleet'.)

Sloane Square is named after Sir Hans Sloane, a wealthy
society physician at the beginning of the eighteenth century,
one-time president of the Royal Society, at one time owner

151

of practically all of the village of Chelsea. His name is memorialized elsewhere: in Sloane Street running northward from Sloane Square, and even in Hans Road, Hans Crescent and Hans Square near Knightsbridge. He lived in Chelsea, in a manor house that had belonged to Henry VIII, and kept a collection of rocks, minerals, stuffed birds and animals, plant specimens, fossils and books that became the foundation of the British Museum. We'll see his statue a little later on this walk.

Before you leave Sloane Square you may want to walk around a little. It is a busy place, with a number of shops and pubs and a hotel, a big department store, and the Royal Court Theatre on the eastern side. The Royal Court occupies an important place in British theatrical history; over the years it has offered new and innovative plays — ones that were unacceptable in West End theatres. Thus many of Shaw's plays were first produced here, and in 1956 John Osborne's *Look Back in Anger* was presented here, an event that marked a totally new direction in post-war theatre. Most recently, it has been the home of a women's theatre group, devoted to putting on both old and new plays written by women.

When you leave Sloane Square, take King's Road to the west, past the large department store, Peter Jones. King's Road is now the main shopping thoroughfare of Chelsea, with antique shops, small and exclusive clothing stores — especially for the young — and lots of restaurants and pubs, but it was named because it was the direct route used by Charles II and later monarchs from their London residences to Hampton Court.

Most of Chelsea's most interesting residential areas are south of King's Road, towards the river, and these are still desirable and expensive places to live. We'll walk through those areas and come back later to the shopping district.

Turn left at either Walpole Street or Royal Avenue, both of which will lead you to St Leonard's Terrace, where you will have to backtrack a little to Franklin's Row before you continue south to Royal Hospital Road. Almost at once, when you leave King's Road, you will be in an area of pleasant, mostly eighteenth-century houses, places where many famous people have lived. Bram Stoker, for example, the author of *Dracula*, lived in St Leonard's Terrace and so did Sir Laurence Olivier, at No. 7.

But the first major objective of this walk is the Royal Hospital, founded by Charles II in 1682 as a retirement home for soldiers, and built by Christopher Wren. The hospital is still used for this purpose; some 450 pensioners live there, wearing their easily recognizable scarlet coats in summertime, more subdued dark blue coats in the winter. One of them will probably be your guide when you visit the hospital; he is likely to expect a small tip at the end of the tour, as his pension is very small.

The principal building is an open square, facing the river across an expanse of beautifully landscaped gardens. As you enter from Royal Hospital Road, Wren's chapel is to the left of the entry way, and the Great Hall, used as a dining-room, is on your right. Both rooms are open to the public. In the middle of the square, is Figure Court, with a Grinling Gibbons statue of Charles II in Roman toga. On Founder's Day, in May, the pensioners gather in the court, wearing their red outfits to mark the change of seasons, and give three cheers for Charles, waving their three-cornered hats in the air.

The gardens behind the hospital, which stretch all the

CHELSEA COLLEGE AND THE ROTUNDA IN RANELAGH GARDENS

way to the river, are pleasant for taking a stroll. To the east lies the area known as Ranelagh Gardens, presently the site of the Chelsea Flower Show each June, and in the eighteenth century one of the great 'pleasure gardens' of the town to which everyone flocked for tea and dalliance on sunny summer days, usually arriving by river. The great rotunda, Ranelagh's most famous structure, has long since disappeared.

When you have seen enough of the hospital and grounds, our walk will continue west on Royal Hospital Road. Almost immediately you will pass the National Army Museum, which provides a history of the British Army from 1485 to 1914. Then you will reach Tite Street, where we are in the heart of the most interesting residential areas of Chelsea.

Turn left on Tite Street. No. 34 was once the residence of Oscar Wilde; it was here that he enjoyed his early popularity and it was here that he was arrested for homo-sexuality, which was still a crime in the late nineteenth century. Also along Tite Street the American-born painter, John Singer Sargent, had his studio; so did Augustus John. The American painter James McNeill Whistler tried to build a house here, but a disastrous law suit forced him to sell before it was completed.

Turn right along Dilke Street just before you come to the noisy and busy Embankment, glance up some of the charming residential streets to your right and, when Dilke Street ends at Swan Walk, turn right again. The wall on your left here surrounds the Chelsea Physic Garden, established by the Apothecaries' Society in 1673. The land was owned by Sir Hans Sloane, who deeded it to the society; in gratitude they put a statue of Sloane in the centre of the garden. You can see it from any one of the gates. For years the garden was not open to the public, but recently it has changed its policy to admit the public on Wednesday and Sunday afternoons. Hundreds of medicinal herbs grow here, including some which are quite rare and beautiful.

A little further east, Royal Hospital Road leads into the Chelsea Embankment, but if you bear to the right at this point you will find yourself in Cheyne (pronounced

154

CHEYNE WALK

'chainy') Walk, a street of lovely eighteenth-century houses facing the river. Some of Chelsea's writers and artists lived here, but now the houses are too expensive — only bankers and business executives can afford them.

No. 16, known as the Queen's House, was the residence of Dante Gabriel Rossetti, the nineteenth-century poet and painter. He kept a regular menagerie at the back — hedgehogs, wombats, wallabies, kangaroos, peacocks, a chameleon and even a laughing jackass. They kept escaping from their cages, much to the annoyance of his neighbours; ever since, all leases in Cheyne Walk contain a provision against the keeping of wild animals.

If you go up Cheyne Row you will soon come to No. 24, which was the home of Thomas and Jane Carlyle. It has been restored as nearly as possible to the way it looked when Carlyle lived there, and a visit will give you a good sense of how a nineteenth-century gentleman of modest means lived. On the top floor is the soundproof study that Carlyle had built so that he could work without distraction and in the living-room is the chair in which he was sitting when he died. The pleasant but small garden at the back is where Carlyle went out to smoke, because his wife Jane would not allow smoking in her house.

Back to Cheyne Walk, on the corner stands the King's Head and Eight Bells, a fine old riverfront pub with excellent lunches. There are several others in the neighbourhood, all of them placed close to the river because they were built at a time when most travellers to Chelsea arrived by boat. This might be a good place to take a rest and have a snack before proceeding.

As you continue along Cheyne Walk, you will be in the area of Chelsea in which Henry VIII had his manor house, built not long after he had ordered the execution of his good friend and neighbour, Sir Thomas More. We'll see a statue of More a little further along in front of the church where he preached, Chelsea Old Church. Parts of this church are very old, but most of it is new, since it was badly damaged in the Second World War. There is a memorial to Sir Thomas More inside, but no one knows for sure where his body is buried. His head was cut off and displayed on a spike as a warning to other traitors; it was later interred at Canterbury.

Sir Thomas More was the friend and confidant of Henry VIII, who often visited him in Chelsea, but More refused to sanction Henry's marriage to Anne Boleyn. With typical directness, Henry won the argument by cutting off his friend's head. And then, less than a year later, he also cut off Anne Boleyn's head, so he could marry his new favourite, Jane Seymour.

If you continue up Old Church Street, you will soon find your way back to King's Road, now at its western end, about three-quarters of a mile from where you started out in Sloane Square. If you still have energy, the walk back along King's Road is fascinating — not just for its history places, but for the people themselves. Chelsea has always been known for its nonconformists and the young people who walk along King's Road today are maintaining the old tradition.

The shops, too, provide interest of their own, with something for everyone. And of course there are always plenty of small cafés along the way where you can stop for rest and sustenance.

But if you want to end the walk without going back to Sloane Square, you will need to catch a bus on King's Road: No. 11, 19, 22 or 49. Check your bus map — if you get on a bus before Chelsea Town Hall, near Sydney Street, you will be outside the Central Zone and you may have to pay a supplement if you have the limited pass. The No. 49 goes up Sydney Street to South Kensington and then east. Nos. 19 and 22 go to Hyde Park Corner and Piccadilly Circus and to Holborn. The No. 11 goes to the City via Victoria Station and Trafalgar Square. If you walk back to Sloane Square you will find an Underground station there as well.

To build, to plant, whatever you intend,
To rear the Column, or the Arch to bend,
To swell the Terras, or to sink the Grot;
In all, let Nature never be forgot.
But treat the Goddess like a modest fair,
Nor over-dress, nor leave her wholly bare;
Let not each beauty ev'ry where be spy'd,
Where half the skill is decently to hide.
He gains all points, who pleasingly confounds,
Surprizes, varies, and conceals the Bounds.

Alexander Pope

THIS IS a fairly long walk up the river, one that will take most of a day. We'll go to Hammersmith first, originally a quiet little fishing village, but important because it was on the main road out of London heading for Bath, Bristol, Exeter and Plymouth and especially important to the king and his court because it lay on the road to the palace at Richmond. Thus many important inns appeared here in the eighteenth century and many wealthy people chose to build country villas here. Today, we can remember some of the stories of those people as we bask in the river views, enjoy two or three fine old pubs, visit Hogarth's house and Chiswick House, the latter one of the most interesting and surely the most original of those country villas.

Getting to our starting point is easy: take either the Piccadilly or District lines to Hammersmith; this stop is outside the Central Zone, so if you have a pass you will have to pay a supplementary fare as you leave the station. Hammersmith Broadway does not seem like a village today; it looks like the city centre of any modern town, with

158

shops and public buildings, hotels and theatres. The Lyric Theatre, Hammersmith, often produces interesting contemporary plays.

The first task, then, will be to get yourself oriented, for you will need to find your way out of this busy place in a southerly direction, to get to the river and relative quiet where you can gain a sense of history.

On the western edge of Hammersmith Broadway is Queen Caroline Street, going south. This street is the only monument to a scandalous queen — Caroline, the wife of 'Prinny' (see Walk No. 15), son of George III who later became George IV.

'Prinny' married Caroline because his father promised to pay off his gambling debts if he did so. She had to share her honeymoon with one of her husband's mistresses, but she soon established herself as a worthy partner to the faithless Prince of Wales. She took her Italian servant, Bergami, as her lover and lived with him openly.

'Prinny' tried to divorce her when his father died and he became king, but he was unable to push the divorce bill through the House of Lords, even though there was a notorious trial in which her indiscretions were publicized widely. Later, when George was to be crowned in Westminster Abbey, he refused to allow her to be crowned queen; she tried to attend as a spectator but was turned away at the door.

Oddly enough, the citizens of Hammersmith, where she had chosen to live and where she later retired, saw her as something of a martyr and cheered her when she drove through the streets in her coach. After the coronation episode, though, public sympathy waned even in Hammersmith, as this little verse testifies:

> Gracious Queen, we thee implore:
> Go away, and sin no more.
> Or, if the effort be too great,
> Go away, at any rate.

To everyone's surprise, Caroline took the advice and died very soon after the coronation. The house where she lived, near the river, has disappeared, but this street remains a memorial to a lively if dissolute queen. And it will lead you in a very short distance to the place where she used to live, on the edge of the river, with magnificent views up and down stream. Though the house is gone, the views remain for you to enjoy today.

You'll find yourself on the river walk, here called Lower Mall, just at the Hammersmith Bridge. Turn right, or up river, and you will soon pass some splendid eighteenth-century houses, with some fine iron grill work. These were residences of the gentry when they were built, made attractive by the view and by the quiet village atmosphere that surrounded them. They are still expensive and desirable residences for the same reasons.

Within the first block you will pass several pleasant waterfront pubs, the Blue Anchor and the Rutland, but if you have started this walk in the morning they will probably not yet be open. Not much further along you will pass, at a point where the walkway narrows, the Dove, a famous old pub with a pleasant deck out over the water. James Thompson, the eighteenth-century poet, visited here and is reputed to have written several stanzas of his long poem, *The Seasons*, in an upstairs room.

The narrow road changes its name along the way, becoming Furnival Gardens and then Upper Mall, eventually Chiswick Mall, but as long as you follow the river upstream you can't get lost and you will always have pleasant views, with interesting gardens and houses.

For example, soon after you pass the Dove, you will see Kelmscott House, where William Morris, the nineteenth-century artist and craftsman, had his studio. If you walk a few yards up the driveway you should be able to find the plaque that urges you to 'Drink a glass' in memory of the lecture hall that stood here — and presumably the thirsty listeners.

It's worth remembering, too, as we walk along this charming street, that Hammersmith has been home to royalty for a long time — even before Caroline. Catherine of Braganza, Charles II's queen in the late seventeenth century, was a staunch Roman Catholic from Portugal who was heartily disliked by most of the English. She found a haven in Hammersmith, which at that time had a large Catholic community.

Catherine was a rather simple woman, who genuinely loved Charles and who could not be reconciled to her easygoing husband's many mistresses. Hence she built a house in Hammersmith and spent much time here in the latter years of her life, even after Charles died, before she finally returned to her native Portugal. But unlike the less decorous Caroline, Catherine of Braganza does not even seem to have a street named after her — such are the rewards of virtue.

As you continue along Upper Mall, you will note a number of small sailing and rowing clubs, each with its own landing jetty and distinctive pennant. One of those you may have noticed is the Furnival Club, named after its founder, Dr Furnival, a scholarly gentleman with a long white beard who rowed regularly until a very old age. He is supposed to be the first man to teach women to row, and he encouraged them to wear comfortable clothes — bloomers or even shorts. The latter almost got the wearers arrested.

You will pass several more pubs. The Old Ship, right on the waterfront, has a fine garden overlooking the river, and a little further on the Black Lion, away from the river, also has a fine garden. These pubs have been here for a long time, serving the people who lived in this area as well as those who sailed up and down the river.

Soon you will note that the walk you are following now is called Chiswick Mall (pronounced 'chizzik') and the general appearance changes just a little. The houses facing the river are a little larger, a little grander, and almost all of them have private gardens leading down to the river, often with a landing stage for a small boat. Chiswick was another village in the eighteenth century and its charming, bucolic atmosphere attracted even wealthier citizens to make this their home.

While Hammersmith housed Catherine, Charles II's faithful wife, Chiswick was home to Lady Castlemaine, one of his most notorious and dissolute mistresses. Lady Castlemaine's house is still standing and you will pass it on

Chiswick Mall — it is a lovely brick villa called Walpole House. Some people also claim that Walpole House was a model for Miss Pinkerton's school for young ladies in Thackeray's *Vanity Fair*. There's another contender for that honour that we'll see a bit later.

Lady Castlemaine lived here after she was cast off by the king. But Charles continued to pay her a generous allowance, so she lived well. She may have been wicked, but she did not lack for friends and she retained her beauty well into middle age, as many portraits of her testify. Samuel Pepys, the diarist, admired her tremendously and was always buying miniatures of her portraits that he could take home. You can check for yourself by looking up Kneller's large portrait of her in the National Gallery. In this case, the wages of sin were a pleasant and comfortable old age and a funeral in the parish church at Chiswick with two dukes and four peers as pallbearers.

After you walk past the tip of Chiswick Eyot, a narrow island lying just offshore that becomes a part of the mainland at low tide, you will come to Church Street, leading away from the river. This will soon lead you to another very busy intersection, the Hogarth Roundabout. Just to the left, take a look down a narrow gravelled walk called Chiswick Square at Boston House, a handsome eighteenth-century brick house that is the other possible model for Thackeray's school in *Vanity Fair*.

At the Hogarth Roundabout, almost swallowed up by the traffic, is Hogarth's house, where the painter and engraver lived for five years. It is not easy to find, but if you turn right off Church Street and go through the pedestrian underpass you should be very near it — still on the river side of the principal traffic street, the Great West Road. Hogarth's house is much the same as it was when the painter lived here and it contains many Hogarth prints and books and other memorabilia.

After visiting Hogarth's house you will need to go back the way you came and turn left from Church Street to go down the continuation of Great West Road, here called Burlington Lane after the Earl of Burlington whose Chiswick House we will be visiting in a moment. It is just a

CHISWICK OLD CHURCH

few hundred yards along, on the opposite side of the road.

Alternatively, if you want to go directly from Chiswick Mall and come back a little later to Hogarth's house, you can turn left down a narrow path about halfway up Church Street called Powell's Walk. This will lead you past the churchyard of the Chiswick parish church, where you can find Hogarth's tomb, erected by his friend David Garrick, the actor. It is a large tomb, appearing almost at once on your left. There are other famous people buried here as well — Lady Castlemaine, for example, and James McNeill Whistler, the American-born painter.

Powell's Walk will eventually bring you out on the busy road almost across from Chiswick House. Cross at the signal and walk just a few yards beyond to the entrance.

CHISWICK HOUSE

Chiswick House was built in the early eighteenth century by the Third Earl of Burlington, with the help and advice of his good friend, the poet Alexander Pope. As a young man, Burlington had travelled to Italy and developed a more than amateur interest in architecture, particularly the architecture popularized in the sixteenth century by the Italian Andrea Palladio, whose *Four Books of Architecture* had a profound influence on Burlington and other builders of the time.

Thus the 'Palladian' style, well exemplified by Chiswick House (as well as the Queen's House in Greenwich and the Banqueting House, both by Inigo Jones), became a familiar term applied to buildings of this period. The style is basically classical, with rounded arches, Greek and Roman pillars, domes and a massive, symmetrical appearance, in stone rather than wood — Portland stone for public buildings, brick for private houses.

So Burlington built a Roman villa at Chiswick, not as a residence — he lived in a fine house nearby — but as a 'palace of art', where he could entertain his friends and display his paintings and sculptures. The villa may be visited today. It is now almost completely restored and once again separated from the residential structures that grew up around it in the nineteenth century which obscured its classical style and symmetry. Upstairs, the interior rooms are all finished in different colours, with plenty of gold leaf and elaborate painted ceilings. On the ground floor, more sparsely furnished, are many architect's drawings that provide a history of the structure.

Alexander Pope's part in both the building and the gardens that surround it should not be underestimated. He was a little older than Burlington; besides being a poet he was a painter of some skill and had a considerable knowledge of architecture and landscape architecture. He was living in Chiswick when plans for this house got under way, but later he developed his own estate a short distance up the river at Twickenham on a somewhat more modest scale.

Both Pope and Burlington were preoccupied with the difficult matter of 'taste', which was assumed in the eighteenth century to separate the sophisticated from the vulgar. For both men, 'good taste' meant an appreciation of the past, particularly of the ancient past of Greece and Rome, and a modelling of their own work on the works of the past — although without slavish imitation.

Some scholars have called this age 'neo-classic'; Pope himself would probably have preferred 'Augustan', after the Emperor Augustus Caesar who lived in Rome at the time of Christ in an elegant, sophisticated court. Pope wrote a poetic epistle, 'On Taste', which he addressed to his friend Burlington, which praised those classical efforts his friend was making at Chiswick and in his town house in London — along Piccadilly, now the home of the Royal Academy of Art (see Walk No. 5). Lines from that epistle give us the epigraph for this walk.

There's a great deal of eighteenth-century aesthetic theory implied in those ten lines, including the important dictum of moderation — not too much of even a good thing. 'Nature' in this case becomes almost a synonym of that quality, but it means many other things as well—propriety, decorum, style. Still, Pope was best as a satirist, tearing down the awful rather than praising the good; you can get an even better notion of what he and Burlington were aiming at by reading his long description in the same epistle of 'Timon's villa', an imaginary house built by a man with lots of money and no 'taste' whatsoever.

But if Pope could sometimes get uncomfortably profound, remember too that he could also be playful, as in the lines that precede our next walk, No. 20. He produced a charming little dialogue about the gateway you can see in the garden of Chiswick House, a gateway that leads nowhere. It was originally designed by Inigo Jones and given to the Earl of Burlington by Sir Hans Sloane (see Walk No. 18). Here is what Pope wrote:

> Oh gate, how com'st thou here?
>   I was brought from Chelsea last year,
> Battered with wind and weather;
>   Inigo Jones put me together,
> Sir Hans Sloane
>   Let me alone,
> Burlington brought me hither.

At any rate, visit Chiswick House and grounds, and compare your 'taste' with that of the earl and his friend the poet. Whatever else you conclude, you will probably find it a strange and wonderful building to appear on an English country estate and perhaps you can imagine how the villagers of the time might have believed that the gentry were a little out of touch with reality. Not that the villagers would ever have been invited inside — we must consider ourselves fortunate.

Now it is time to return after a fairly long walk and probably a long day. Returning isn't easy, since we are rather out in the country, where the Underground stations are few and far between. Your best bet, if you don't want to go back the way you came, is to walk back to the Hogarth Roundabout. Visit the painter's house, if you haven't already done so, and then walk north along Devonshire

Road to Chiswick High Street. Here you can catch a local bus going east that will take you as far as Hammersmith Broadway. Or you can continue north via Turnham Green to the Turnham Green Underground station, which is on the District line.

Kew Gardens

'I am his Highness' dog at Kew,
Pray tell me, Sir, whose dog are you?'

Alexander Pope

THIS IS another walk for a sunny day, for a day when you have had enough of the city pavements and long for green grass and flowers. On a summer Sunday, you will be joining throngs of London families for an outing, but Kew Gardens — more properly the Royal Botanic Gardens at Kew — include almost 300 acres, so you will not feel crowded. Wear comfortable clothes, be sure to take your camera, as well as binoculars if you fancy some bird-watching, and prepare to spend a day in the country, although it is a very short trip from central London.

Like the last walk, Kew is up river from London and right on the Thames, so the most romantic way of getting there, and the slowest, is by river steamer. Boats leave from Westminster Pier every half hour during the summer and take about an hour and a half. Perhaps the best time to take the boat is on the return journey, when you are tired from walking and a long leisurely ride seems in order.

A much quicker way to Kew is by Underground or bus. Kew Gardens station is on the District line, but outside the Central Zone. Make sure you get on a train heading for Richmond; other trains may go to Ealing Broadway or Wimbledon. It is about a five-minute walk from the station to Victoria Gate.

To come by bus you will need to catch a No. 27, which runs east along Marylebone Road, past Notting Hill Gate, down Kensington Church Street and then west along Kensington High Street. The bus is much slower than the Underground, of course, but it is a pleasant ride and it will take you through parts of London that you may not have seen before. Sometimes when you are taking a new bus trip, it is interesting to follow the route on your map — it's also a good way to strike up a conversation with your fellow travellers. Of course, if you have only a map of central London, you'll be off the edge by the time you get to Kew.

You can get off the bus just after crossing Kew Bridge, which will be close to the main gate to the gardens and close to the palace, or you can ask the driver to let you off at Victoria Gate — the bus stops almost in front.

You will find much to see and do inside Kew Gardens; it would be unreasonable here to prescribe a specific route. Rather, we'll provide a little historical background, mention some of the most interesting sights and let you wander through according to your own inclinations. Good guide books and information pamphlets are available at the bookshop and souvenir stand in the Orangery, just south of Kew Palace.

Kew Gardens have been connected with the royal family only since the mid-eighteenth century, when Princess Augusta, the mother of George III, established a small garden here. Under her direction, William Chambers built the Orangery and the fantastic Chinese Pagoda, both of which are still standing. And Augusta's husband, Prince Frederick, was given a dog by Alexander Pope with the collar inscription that provides the epigraph to this walk.

At one time there were larger and more elaborate royal residences on the grounds, but the only one surviving today is the modest red-brick building near the main entrance called Kew Palace. It was originally built by a Dutch refugee in the early seventeenth century (hence called the 'Dutch House'), and became the principal royal residence at Kew in the late eighteenth century. 'Prinny', whom we have read about in less countrified contexts (see Walks No. 15 and 19), used this as a residence; so did his parents, George III and Queen Charlotte. Perhaps the best description of life at Kew Palace has been given by the young novelist, Fanny

Burney, who spent five rather dull years as Queen Charlotte's Keeper of the Robes. In a letter to her family, Fanny described life at Kew:

The Kew life, you will perceive, is different from the Windsor. As there are no early prayers, the Queen rises later; and as there is no form or ceremony here of any sort, her dress is plain, and the hour for the second toilette extremely uncertain. The Royal family are here always in so very retired a way, that they live as the simplest country gentlefolks. The King has not even an equerry with him, nor the Queen any lady to attend her when she goes her airings.

After you visit the Palace, you may wish to see the Queen's Garden, recently designed as a seventeenth-century kitchen garden, with herbs, vegetables, fruit trees and flowers. Each growing thing is carefully tended and labelled; not only are the plants interesting in themselves, but you may be able to get some idea of the food that was served around three hundred years ago.

Moving south from the palace, the Orangery is just a short distance along the Broad Walk. To the left are a number of glass houses and museums with varying exhibits throughout the year. Ahead is the small pond and, to the right, the imposing Palm House, a greenhouse large enough for full-size trees. It's always very humid inside, but there are plants and trees from all over the world; a gallery some thirty feet up provides an excellent panoramic view.

To the west of the Palm House are some of the rose gardens and, looking south down a long row of tall trees, you can get a distant glimpse of the strangely improbable Pagoda, a tall tower in the Chinese style built by William Chambers. It is an odd thing to find in an English garden, but perhaps not so odd here, since this garden grows plants from all over the world.

South, towards the Pagoda, you will pass the Temperate House, with its rhododendrons, camellias and many other flowers. Nearby you will find a place to refresh yourself — both a small café with tables set up outside and a somewhat more formal but still inexpensive restaurant inside.

To continue our roughly clockwise tour of the gardens, in the far south-west corner is the Queen's Cottage, a delightful small thatched roof building where the court ladies went when they tired of formality to play at being milkmaids. Near the cottage is an area of the park where you cannot walk — an area that has been allowed to revert completely to its natural state. It is pleasant to walk along its verge and admire the wild flowers which seem at certain times of the year more impressive than the carefully cultivated gardens in the rest of the park.

Turning back north, in a short distance you will come to the large lake that dominates the western side of the gardens and, a little further to the west, the Thames, with some pleasant country views. In the distance, across the river, you can see Syon House, a beautiful Robert Adam mansion dating from 1760. Although it is the residence of the Duke of Northumberland, it is open to the public.

To get back to the starting point, you can choose either to walk along the river or to go to the east side of the lake and walk through the more cultivated part of the gardens. There are many walks and enough signs and maps to keep you from getting lost. You will find things to see and do that will keep you busy for the rest of this day and perhaps others, if you choose to return. For many Londoners, no spring season is complete without a visit to Kew, when the flowering trees and bulbs are at their best.

When the time comes to go back, there are the usual choices: a No. 27 bus to Kew Road, either outside Victoria Gate or near Kew Bridge, the Underground at Kew Garden station, about a five-minute walk to the east from Victoria Gate, or a river boat. If you want to take the boat, you must go out of the main gate and turn left down a narrow street called Ferry Lane. It will lead to the river and, when you turn right and go under Kew Bridge, you will find yourself at the pier where the boats for Westminster dock.

Since the Day that King Bladud first found out the bogs,
And thought them so good for himself and his hogs,
Not one of the Faculty ever has try'd
These excellent waters to cure his own hide.

Christopher Anstey

THE LINES above come from a fine satiric poem, 'The New Bath Guide', published in 1766, when Bath was at the height of its popularity as a fashionable resort town. Anstey is referring here to the legend of Bath's founding: Bladud, a prince who was also a swineherd, had been sent from the court as a leper. Seeing his pigs rolling in the warm mud, he tried it himself and was miraculously cured. From then on, according to the legend, Bath's reputation was made.

Of course, whatever the efficacy of the waters, wherever a quick cure is promised there are bound to be quack doctors. In the eighteenth century, Bath had more than its share, as Anstey suggests, who were quick to recommend the mineral waters even though they would never dream of trying them themselves.

Though the story of King Bladud is only a legend, it is indisputable that the Romans discovered the hot springs in the early years of their occupation, and for four centuries they came to the place they named Aquae Sulis, after Sul, one of the local deities. They built not only the elaborate baths, some of which still survive today, but temples and other buildings as well; no doubt the hot mineral waters were soothing to the muscles of war-weary legionnaires.

BEAU NASH

The ladies and gentlemen of the eighteenth century also came ostensibly to take the waters, but they were probably not too concerned about whether they worked or not. They came to Bath mainly for a good time, for coffee drinking and balls and masquerades and assemblies, where they could see and be seen. Everyone seems to have come to Bath in the eighteenth century; in the course of these walks we'll find out about some of these famous visitors, but there were many ordinary citizens as well: London merchants with their wives and daughters, craftsmen and artisans, and country squires. Everyone flocked to the cheerful pleasure city, and duchesses jostled with ladies' maids in the ever-popular Assembly Rooms.

Curiously enough, Bath served England during those days as a kind of school of manners, an arbiter of taste. With such a mixture of social classes, there was bound to be friction, and it was not only the tradesmen's wives who offended against decorum but the duchesses as well. In the early part of the century, Bath was quite a rough place, with much gambling, brawling, duelling, nude bathing, illicit love-making and other unseemly behaviour. The remedy came from an unexpected source.

Richard Nash was a gambler and card sharp who came to Bath early in the century, attracted by the opportunity to find wealthy people with time on their hands. He was a clever man, opportunistic, basically honest, but also arrogant, conceited and snobbish. He soon inherited the role of Master of Ceremonies — an honorary title that had been held by a man who was killed in a duel shortly after Nash arrived — and he held the post for the rest of his life, adding to it the title of King of Bath.

Beau Nash, as he became known, had a passion for propriety. His early efforts clearly improved Bath: he raised money to build better roads and streets, he had concert halls and a theatre and meeting rooms built, he forbade private parties, which got rid of much social snobbery, and he wrote and posted a set of rules for those who attended balls and assemblies. Men, for example, were not to arrive in muddy riding boots; women were not to appear in aprons. He was caustic and direct in his criticism of anyone who dared to disobey him.

He was not afraid to rebuke anyone, no matter how highly placed. The Princess Amelia, daughter of George II, was refused one more dance after eleven o'clock, because that was the hour that Nash had decreed dancing was to cease. She was furious at the time, but she later forgave him and continued to come to Bath. When the Duchess of Queensberry appeared in an apron, he told her harshly that such a costume was suitable only for a lady's maid. She apologized to him and promised never to wear one again.

Perhaps one of Nash's greatest accomplishments was his success in forbidding duelling. Duelling, in the eighteenth century, was a gentleman's vice; pride was a delicate thing and even an imagined slight could lead to a challenge, which of course had to be accepted. Gentlemen wore swords as a matter of course, the way men today wear neckties, and it was easy to pull one out at the climax of a drunken brawl, or to issue a challenge that had to be settled immediately.

Nash solved the problem simply — by banning the wearing of swords in the city. There was much opposition, of course, but as usual he was obeyed. The ban was generally respected, although the urge to duel continued: in

174

Sheridan's play, *The Rivals*, which is set in Bath, when Captain Absolute goes out for his duel, he has to hide his sword under his coat. In the years that followed, the custom of wearing swords gradually declined, not only in Bath but throughout England.

Not everyone appreciated Beau Nash's commands, nor was he universally popular. But in the long run his influence was probably good and, because of the popularity of Bath as a holiday town, because of the thousands of people who came for a visit and took home their new habits, his influence was far-reaching, through a society that was enjoying a new kind of social democracy. Nash never preached morality — even his attack on duelling came from his feeling that the shedding of blood was messy and indecorous; manners and style mattered most to him.

You can see a statue of Beau Nash in the Pump Room and you may visit his grave and monument in the Abbey Church, one of the oldest buildings in the town and the starting point of today's walk. We will cover very little ground, but we will see many of the important older areas of the city, as well as the baths, the Abbey, the Guildhall, the Parade Gardens and beautiful Pultney Bridge. All of these are in the natural valley nestled in the curve of the River Avon where the town was first established. On the second Bath walk, we'll climb the hill to visit the Assembly Rooms and look at the splendid Georgian residential areas for

NEW PUMP ROOM ANNEXE, BATH

175

which Bath is famous.

The Bath Abbey is a late medieval structure, built during the early sixteenth century, but there has been a church structure here since the seventh century. In spite of its magnificence, it is not a cathedral, although it once served that function; Wells is now the nearest cathedral town. But it is a splendid building in a fine setting. It is best viewed from across the paved area to the west, where you can see the fine window and the angels climbing the ladders on either side, as well as the flying buttresses.

The interior of the church has a magnificent fan-vaulted ceiling, a great many monuments to famous people who lived and died in Bath, and a number of fine stained-glass windows, most of which are modern. Because of its many windows, Bath Abbey is often called the 'Lantern of the West'.

From the Abbey, it is only a few steps to the Roman Baths and the Grand Pump Room. The Pump Room, a favourite resort of Bath visitors in the eighteenth century, still offers coffee or tea and sometimes concerts; there is also a fountain with mineral water for drinking, if you enjoy the taste. At one end you can see the fine old Tompion clock that Dickens mentions in *Pickwick Papers*, and in a niche above it stands the statue of Beau Nash, still sternly surveying his guests.

The springs in Bath are the only really hot springs in England; the water flows at the rate of more than half a million gallons a day and is a constant forty-nine degrees Centigrade. It is radioactive and contains many minerals and salts. You can still take therapeutic baths in various establishments around the city.

Perhaps the most interesting place to visit is the Roman Great Bath, which is remarkably well preserved after so many centuries. Archaeologists continue to make excavations in the area and regularly turn up new discoveries. Besides looking at the Great Bath itself, you will have an opportunity to examine the subterranean plumbing methods used by the Romans, and there is a fine museum displaying many of the artefacts that have been unearthed during recent excavations.

While you are walking through this part of Bath, you might wish to stop in the Tourist Information Centre at the western end of the churchyard. Here you can pick up maps and brochures that will assist you in your subsequent explorations of this interesting town and the surrounding countryside.

Now we shall leave the town centre, a place that is usually filled to the brim in the summer with visitors from all over the world, resting their feet and eating snacks from the many shops that surround the Abbey. There is much more to see in Bath and we'll move on into quieter, less crowded parts of the city.

One of the most charming aspects of Bath is the number of narrow streets that are accessible only to walkers. The absence of motor cars is a great boon to the dedicated walker, enabling him or her to concentrate on the views and not worry about traffic. Besides, since so much of the architecture has remained unchanged, it is easy to believe yourself back in another century; in these narrow passageways you almost expect to encounter Beau Nash, the Duchess of Queensberry or an invalid being wheeled to the doctor in his Bath chair. We will only have time to go down a few of these streets on these walks, but there are plenty more, tempting you to explore further on your own.

From the Roman Baths, we will walk through a little of this area, moving first west and then north and then east again, to make a small circle that will give you a chance to plot your own course through some of the pedestrian streets. Begin west along Bath Street, with its pleasant colonnades, where you will soon pass the Cross Bath, and then turn right past the Royal Baths, both of which were popular spas in the eighteenth century.

Left down Westgate Street and right almost at once into Sawclose Street will take you past the Theatre Royal, built in the early nineteenth century, although Bath had its own theatre in the eighteenth century as well. From here, head back east down whatever streets you like until you come to the High Street, a broad but very short avenue running directly north from the Abbey and containing the municipal buildings of Bath.

One of the most interesting of these buildings is the Guildhall, recently renovated, with a fine Banqueting Room that is worth a visit. The room is designed in the Adam style, with magnificent chandeliers; it contains portraits by Reynolds of George III and Queen Charlotte. The north wing of the Guildhall contains the Victoria Art Gallery, which has an interesting collection of paintings and drawings from the eighteenth to the twentieth century, with a special emphasis on artists who lived and worked in Bath.

Leave this area to the south, towards the open space east of the Abbey called the Orange Grove, which was named after William, Prince of Orange, who visited the town in 1734. This area was named in honour of that visit, and the obelisk in the centre was erected by Beau Nash, with an appropriate inscription by the prince's doctor.

The Orange Grove overlooks the Parade Gardens near the river. These gardens are a good place to relax after a day of sightseeing and provide marvellous pastoral views of the River Avon. The entrance is from the North Parade.

Our final goal today is back past the Orange Grove, along the river down the Grand Parade, to Pultney Bridge. Pultney Bridge was built by Robert Adam in the late eighteenth century and it is lined with shops. This is one of the most photographed places in Bath and you will quickly see why.

If you still have enough energy, a walk across Pultney Bridge will lead you to Great Pultney Street, a fine straight thoroughfare that runs for about a quarter of a mile directly to the Holburne Museum and the Sydney Gardens. The museum houses the art collection of Sir Thomas Holburne, which was donated to Bath in the late nineteenth century. It contains some excellent examples of paintings by Gainsborough and Allan Ramsay, also some earlier Dutch, Flemish and German works, as well as rare books.

The gardens behind were laid out in the very late eighteenth century, perhaps as a place of shade and quiet where ladies and gentlemen might repair when the balls and assemblies began to grow wearisome. It was a good place to relax then and it is an appropriate place to end this walk.

Twas a glorious sight to behold the fair sex
All wading with gentlemen up to their necks,
And view them so prettily stumble and sprawl
In a great smoking kettle as big as our hall.

Christopher Anstey

NO DOUBT a great many people came to Bath during its
heyday in the eighteenth century to seek a cure for their
illness through bathing, but perhaps more — as Anstey
suggests above — came to watch and to enjoy both the
ridiculous of ladies and gentlemen dipping themselves in
muddy hot water and the sublime of the concerts and balls
that brought together the wealthy and famous from all over
England. During the middle of the eighteenth century,
everyone who was anyone, in literature, art, politics or high
society, either lived in or visited Bath.

Bath became popular in the late seventeenth century, as
the curative properties of the water became widely
publicized. Royalty led the way and the rest soon followed.
Charles II visited a number of times, bringing sometimes a
wife and sometimes a mistress. His brother, James II, also
came to the town, as did his daughter, later Queen Anne, in
order to cure her gout; there is no record of whether or not
she succeeded. Naturally the court follower Samuel Pepys
made the pilgrimage, enjoying the sight of the pretty ladies
in the bath with him, but expressing doubts all the same. 'It
cannot be clean,' he wrote in his diary, 'to go so many bodies
together in the same water.' As Swift put it a few years later,
'Everyone is going to Bath.'

Many of the buildings of Bath that we see today were
erected in the later eighteenth century, following general

designs set out by an architect named John Wood. Wood came to Bath in the 1720s and immediately saw an unsurpassed opportunity for city planning. Here was a city on the verge of explosive growth, popular among the wealthy, desperately in need of the amenities that architecture could offer — houses, meeting rooms, hotels and places to dine. To an ambitious young architect it was a heaven-sent opportunity.

Wood was deeply interested in and influenced by the work of the Italian architect Palladio, just as Inigo Jones and Christopher Wren had been. In a way, the clean lines and the symmetry of Palladian architecture echo in stone some of the ideals of Beau Nash in deportment; both suggest an ordered world, one in which elegance and propriety are the most important things, a world without much fanciful decoration or unwelcome surprise. Wood envisaged a whole city built to such a plan.

Such an ambitious goal was perhaps doomed to failure, but Wood succeeded in leaving his mark firmly on the streets of Bath. And the architects who followed him, including his son, who became known as John Wood the Younger, to some extent matched his style and helped to carry out his ideas.

As many writers visited Bath, it was natural that the city should appear in their books. To get a view of Bath in its heyday you should read Smollett's *Humphry Clinker* or the novels of Fanny Burney. Jane Austen lived here for a while, but did not like it, as she was by nature a reclusive person, but the town features as an attractive place in her books. Henry Fielding was often a guest of the wealthy businessman and philanthropist, Ralph Allen, who lived in Bath and encouraged its growth. Although Fielding did not set any of his novels in Bath, he modelled Squire Allworthy, in *Tom Jones*, on the character of his benefactor. In the nineteenth century, both Thackeray and Dickens visited the city and used it as a setting in their writing. Bath was popular not only in real life but in fiction as well.

Now it is time to visit some of the magnificent residential areas of Bath that make the city one of the most imposing examples of Georgian town planning. Much has changed since the eighteenth century, but Bath, unlike many other towns, has developed little industry, so the older buildings have not been pulled down to make way for factories, warehouses and offices. The town remains a spa, a pleasure palace, a place for visitors.

Unfortunately there are sometimes so many visitors that they threaten to overwhelm Bath's quiet dignity. Driving a car there in summer is very ill advised. The narrow streets, most of them one way, often with steep hills and sharp curves, are a motorist's nightmare; walking is by far the best way to see the town. If climbing up the hills is really difficult for you, there is a shuttle bus which goes from the Roman Baths up to the Assembly Rooms at regular intervals.

We'll begin at one of the places we visited near the end of our previous walk, Pultney Bridge. We'll proceed west down Bridge Street and then go along Upper Borough Walls, not a very interesting street in itself, but after a short distance we will pass, on the left, the massive front of the Royal National Hospital for Rheumatic Diseases, one of John Wood the Elder's earliest buildings in Bath, begun in 1738.

The history of this hospital is fascinating. Nash, who was very good at collecting money for worthy causes, helped to raise the amount necessary to build it. Ralph Allen, probably the wealthiest man in Bath, who had made most of his money by quarrying the stone that was used in the town buildings, donated the stone for the hospital, as well as funds. John Wood was its architect. Originally called the Mineral Water Hospital, it was planned for the many indigent sick people who travelled to Bath to try the waters. For more than a century, no Bath resident was treated there. Its ongoing financing came from fines for illegal gambling.

Just beyond the hospital, we will turn right along Queen Street, a charming narrow eighteenth-century street, lined with lovely houses built by the architects who followed John Wood. Queen Street leads to Wood Street, and a left turn will take us to Queen Square, the masterpiece of John Wood the Elder and the only row of terraced houses that he lived to see completed.

QUEEN CAROLINE

Queen Square was named after Queen Caroline, the wife of George II, and, although it was not completed to John Wood's master plan, the north frontage, which is intended to dominate the square the way a palace might dominate the surrounding houses, is still just as Wood designed it; it is one of the finest groups of houses you will see anywhere in the country.

Wood designed this vast façade, which comprises a considerable number of houses, and then farmed out the building of the interiors to a number of contractors. Thus each house is different inside, but all their façades combine to achieve the palace-like effect of Wood's grand design.

You may like to walk around the square, in order to get different views of the splendid north front. The east and west wings were never completed by Wood, nor was the south, all of which were intended to be subsidiary to the northern row. The centre of the square originally contained a garden, long since disappeared, but the obelisk in the centre was erected by Wood to honour the Prince and Princess of Wales. It matches the one we have already seen in the previous walk at the Orange Grove. Wood showed his satisfaction with his design by moving into the centre house of the north group, where he lived for a number of years.

From here we'll walk north down Gay Street (at the north-east corner of Queen Square), named after Robert Gay, a surgeon and wealthy landowner who had leased the area of Queen Square to John Wood. Gay Street, itself lined with splendid eighteenth-century houses, leads directly to The Circus, the last of John Wood's great plans, which he designed but did not live to see completed.

Wood died in 1754, shortly after work began on The Circus. It is clearly one of his Roman plans, built like the Colosseum, but facing inward rather than outward. The plan is simple but brilliant: three separate streets enter The Circus and each faces one of the three segments of symmetrical houses. Originally, the centre was paved; the trees that are there now obstruct the view that Wood intended. There have been some changes in the house façades over the years, but in general the plan remains as Wood intended.

John Wood the Younger completed The Circus according to his father's plans, but after his father's death the son continued his own work as Bath architect. He was responsible for the Royal Crescent, certainly Bath's most spectacular terrace, which we will visit next.

We will go west from The Circus, along Brock Street, also designed by John Wood the Younger. This was intended as the entrance to the Royal Crescent and the houses are designed in a much simpler manner, almost as if to prepare the walker for the first spectacular sight at the top. The Royal Crescent, seen from Brock Street, is a tremendous curving range of buildings to the right, some thirty large houses, fifty feet high, with tremendous columns that start above the first storey. To the left the great expanse of parkway slopes down to the river. Because the Royal Crescent is nearly at the top of the hill, the whole panorama from Brock Street is somehow framed between sky and grass. Walter Ison, a twentieth-century architectural critic, maintains that the Royal Crescent is 'the greatest single achievement in the whole field of our urban architecture'.

The Royal Crescent was built in eight years, in the manner of the other terraces we have already seen: Wood designed the frontage, various builders completed the houses behind. They are still highly desirable residences; many of the ground floors are rented as office space. But No. 1, the first house on your right as you enter from Brock Street, is furnished in the Georgian style and open to the public, so that you may walk through the rooms and imagine what it would have been like to visit Bath in the late eighteenth century.

The Royal Crescent is clearly the masterpiece of John Wood the Younger and the most impressive group of residential houses in Bath, but we have one more important visit to make on this walk, to the 'new' Assembly Rooms, also designed by John Wood the Younger, completed in 1771. To get there, we'll retrace our steps down Brock Street, but about halfway to The Circus turn left at Margaret's Buildings, a pedestrian walkway, and then turn right to follow Circus Mews around to the Assembly Rooms. On the left, where Circus Mews itself turns right, you will pass the Carriage Museum, which is well worth a visit if you are curious about how people travelled in the eighteenth century. It is full of phaetons, curricles, stage coaches, barouches, hansom cabs and other vehicles that brought the rich and sick to Bath and conveyed them up and down the hill, to contribute to what was even then a monumental traffic jam.

The Assembly Rooms do not look particularly impressive from the outside — they may even appear somewhat grim and forbidding. But inside they symbolize better than anything else the gaiety and glamour that was Bath in its heyday.

The Assembly Rooms were where people gathered for balls, for card playing, for concerts and for tea. There had been such rooms in Bath before this one was built—two, in fact, both of them down the hill near the Pump Room, which was the central area of Bath in the early eighteenth century. But after the mid-century, as Bath expanded tremendously in population, the centre moved north, up the hill, into the squares and crescents we have seen, and rooms were needed that were more convenient to all the fine new residences.

Thus John Wood designed these new rooms, which were so successful once they were opened that both of the older rooms below were soon closed. Since then, however, the Assembly Rooms have undergone various transformations. In the early part of the twentieth century they were used for other purposes and much of the splendid interior was damaged. Rebuilt in the 1940s, they were largely destroyed during an air raid in the Second World War, but since then they have once again been rebuilt, carefully modelled after their original style.

Perhaps the most spectacular room now is the great ballroom, more than a hundred feet long and proportionately high, with a curved ceiling and five of the original magnificent chandeliers — they were taken down and stored during the Second World War. There is also a raised recess where musicians played for dancing. Empty now except for tourists, it is easy to imagine how the ballroom might have looked during the 1770s, with elegantly dressed ladies and gentlemen filling the cavernous space.

You can get an even better idea how the ballroom would have looked by visiting the Museum of Costume, which is housed under the Assembly Rooms. The costumes shown cover the period from the late sixteenth century to the present, including many of the brocades and velvets worn in the days when the rooms were first built. There is also a collection of underwear, so you can get some idea of the complexities involved in getting ready for a ball, and displays of jewellery and children's costumes and toys. It is a fine collection, and some of the most interesting items are from our recent past, the early and middle years of the twentieth century, the clothes our parents and grandparents wore.

Now we shall walk down the hill by a different route to see some more of the city. From the Assembly Rooms you must work your way south to George Street, via any of the small streets; at George Street find Milsom Street to continue southward.

Milsom Street, like Gay Street, was named after the owner of the land on which it was built. The street was laid out in the late eighteenth century; it was one of the new streets running up the hill designed to handle the traffic between the Assembly Rooms and the baths. Most of the houses along here are in the Palladian style. On your left, soon after George Street, is a fine group of five houses called Somersetshire Buildings, designed by Thomas Baldwin, one of the young architects who contributed a great deal to Bath towards the end of the eighteenth century. And almost at once after Somersetshire Buildings is a narrow entrance that will lead you back to the Octagon, now run as a museum and gallery by the Royal Photographic Society, called the National Centre of Photography.

In 1767 the Octagon was designed as a 'proprietary' chapel, reflecting an interesting plan devised in wealthy residential areas to provide a private place for worship. Such chapels were run for profit; the very expensive pew rents kept out the riff-raff and the entrepreneurs could afford to hire excellent musicians and preachers. Because they were not consecrated buildings, the chapels did not offer communion services, but they provided an exclusive religious meeting place for the rich people of the neighbourhood.

From here, Milsom Street continues south, and soon you will find yourself in Upper Borough Walls, nearly back at the place where this walk began. There is of course much more to be seen in Bath and its vicinity. Armed with a good map from the Information Centre, you can chart your own course through some more of these attractive streets and you will surely find new and different adventures.

The learn'd in schools, where knowledge first began,
Studies with care th' anatomy of man;
Sees virtue, vice, and passions in their cause,
And fame from science, not from fortune, draws.

John Dryden

THE TOWN of Oxford, with its great and ancient university, lies about fifty miles west of London and it is well worth a day or two of the traveller's time. There are frequent buses and trains to take you there. If you wish to stay overnight, most travel agents will be glad to make arrangements for you, or you could consult some of booklets listing 'bed and breakfasts' and make your own reservations by phone.

Though the town of Oxford is nicely compact, this tour has been divided into two sections, for there is much to see. It is possible to do both walks in a single day, but bear in mind that many of the colleges are open only during afternoon hours; also be selective, for there are thirty-four of them.

We will begin with a walk that centres on the main university buildings, together with some of the colleges near by. Distances are not great and considerable time is spent indoors, so this walk is quite suitable for a showery day. If the weather is good, you may like to tackle the next walk first, for much of it takes you along the meadows and rivers that give the town much of its unforgettable character.

To begin, you will get off the train or bus near the western boundary of our walks. From the railway station, a longish walk down Park End Street and New Road (past the Mound, a remnant of the old castle site) to Queen Street will take you to Carfax Tower and the major intersection of Oxford. From the bus station, head east along George Street, past the New Theatre, until you come to Cornmarket Street, where a right turn will lead to Carfax Tower. Continue south for a few yards to the Information Centre, where you can purchase a city map for a small sum.

Looking at your map, note the area bounded by the High Street on the south, Turl Street on the west, Broad Street on the north and Catte Street on the east. Here, densely situated, are the institutions which form the heart of the university: St Mary's Church, Radcliffe Camera, Bodleian Old Library, the Sheldonian Theatre and the Clarendon Building.

Return to the Carfax intersection now and turn right along the High Street, or 'The High' as it is commonly called

HIGH STREET, OXFORD

188

by the students. As you walk along, you will notice the kinds of shops and cafés that cater for the students — stationery shops, grocers and clothes shops — and you will usually find them busy with their regular customers. But the High Street merchants are aware that more affluent visitors may pass by, so you will also find antiques, rare books and fine prints on sale.

Past Turl Street, Brasenose College is on your left. On the corner of Oriel Street to the right, you will see some of the buildings of Oriel College, while across the High Street from them is the church of St Mary, otherwise known as the University Church. Enter from the High Street and explore the interior; every Sunday during term time the University Sermon is preached.

Famous men have occupied this pulpit: in the eighteenth century, John Wesley railed against the complacency of the Anglican clergy in the face of the terrible living conditions of factory workers and the poor; later he founded the Methodist Church. Oxford pupils found his two-hour sermons too long and priggish; their nickname of 'Methodists' for him and his few followers was a term of abuse.

John Newman, vicar of St Mary's in the last century, used to pack the church with his controversial sermons on the role of the established Church. Eventually, he broke with many of his friends at Oxford when he joined the Roman Catholic Church, but the effect of his influence was to loosen for ever the ties between the Church of England clergy and the university. Up to that time, Oxford was thought of as the place where prospective Anglican clerics were to be educated.

In the eighteenth century, the university was hardly looked upon as a place of learning at all, in spite of John Dryden's assertions. Students caroused in public houses with their teachers; lectures were said to be disgraceful exhibitions of conceit and ignorance; and many students bragged that they never attended lectures or tutoring sessions. But reforms eventually came and with them the respected reputation which an Oxford degree now confers.

The spire of St Mary's rises 188 feet to an excellent

vantage point from which to view the city; it is worth the climb and the small fee. Leave by the north entrance opposite the one you entered by and walk straight on to the round domed Radcliffe Camera. ('Camera', in its old sense, means simply 'room'.) By comparing the church and the Camera you can appreciate the fundamental differences between fourteenth- and eighteenth-century architecture, the former with its 'dreaming spires' symbolising the Age of Faith, the other with its neo-classical proportions representing the Age of Reason.

Said to be the third largest dome in England, the Camera was founded by Dr John Radcliffe, the court physician, as a library for the sciences. James Gibbs, better known for his church that stands in London's Trafalgar Square, St Martin-in-the-Fields, completed the massive building in 1748, but the Science Library has now been moved to other quarters. Today the Radcliffe Camera serves as a reading room for the Bodleian Library next door; books from that building are conveyed by means of an ingenious belt system through a tunnel under the pavement between them. Now and then the Camera serves another purpose — when daring undergraduates find a way to plant a flag on top of

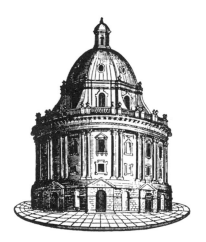

RADCLIFFE CAMERA

the slippery dome.

Though the Camera is closed to non-students, the Bodleian offers a changing exhibition of items from its ancient and valuable collection of books and documents. It is named after Thomas Bodley, who presented the university with his own extensive library in 1602. Today it is one of the six libraries in the country that gets a free copy of every book published in the United Kingdom. It houses more than two and a half million volumes, and over 50,000 manuscripts.

The rooms of the library which are open to visitors include the old ground floor of Duke Humphrey's Library, which now serves as a lobby and book shop. Here one can find unusual souvenirs and gifts, such as an illuminated letters colouring book and a Bodleian Library T-shirt, as well as more scholarly pamphlets, books, prints and slides.

Next comes the Divinity School room, a beautiful chamber built in the fifteenth century. Notice the vaulted ceiling, which is characteristic of that period, in the Perpendicular Gothic style. Have a look at the exhibition cases with their priceless treasures including early works by Shakespeare, letters and manuscripts by familiar English writers, and the first books to be printed in England. Duke Humphrey's Library upstairs is not open to the general public so you will only be able to see pictures or slides of it with its elaborately carved ceiling panels and bosses. The duke was the brother of Henry V and gave his collection of manuscripts to the library. Unfortunately they did not remain there for long, for in 1550, just sixty years later, they were destroyed or dispersed by order of Edward VI.

When you leave the library quadrangle, still heading north, you will find yourself facing the Clarendon Building, the former home of the Oxford Press, and the rather strange-looking Sheldonian Theatre, half round and half rectangle, with its octagonal cupola perched on top. At one time the theatre housed the university printing press, but more recently its chief function has been to provide an auditorium for the important secular assemblies of the university, such as the granting of degrees and other honours.

Gilbert Sheldon, an Oxford clergyman and later Archbishop of Canterbury, thought that the ceremonies were becoming too rowdy for St Mary's church, so he donated money for a new building. A young Professor of Astronomy was given the task of designing and erecting it. He took as his inspiration pictures he had seen of the Theatre of Marcellus in Rome. The name of the professor was Christopher Wren. We must not blame Wren for the faintly ridiculous-looking topknot of the theatre — that was added later by another, less talented builder.

Enter to see the ingenious architecture and the ceiling painting which gives the effect of a tent covering an open-air theatre. If you like, you can climb to the cupola and admire the 360-degree view of Oxford. As you leave the theatre, you will find that along its front railing facing Broad Street are set a number of carved stone heads. They have been restored several times, most recently in 1971; nobody seems to have a very clear idea of whom they represent.

Across the street is the New Bodleian Library building, connected by underground passage to the main building. Now walk west along 'The Broad' to have a look at the many bookshops; Blackwell's is the most well known. There are plenty of eating places and pubs, too, around here, so if you are hungry or thirsty, join the throngs of undergraduates who patronize them.

Now it is time to visit a few of the colleges which share this central area with the university buildings. Retrace your steps to the corner where the Clarendon Building is situated, the intersection of Broad and Catte Streets. Walking a few yards along 'The Catte' towards The High, you will see a famous structure arching over narrow New College Lane. This is a replica of the Italian Bridge of Sighs. It was built in the first part of the twentieth century, connecting the two parts of Hertford College. It is a familiar landmark for those television viewers who watched the BBC production of Evelyn Waugh's *Brideshead Revisited*. Waugh in fact attended Hertford College.

Turn down New College Lane, noticing the ancient walls and buildings as you pass. Some of them date from the fourteenth century. As you avoid the bicycles ridden by undergraduates, black robes flapping about their legs, you can reflect on the remarkable continuity of this scholarly community where the academic torch has been handed down through more than seven centuries. The medieval character of Oxford manifests itself at many unexpected moments.

The organization of the university still reflects the medieval practice of a group of separate and sometimes only loosely associated colleges (or houses, as they are sometimes called), which grant degrees in common, but where the curricula leading up to those degrees may take quite different shapes, depending upon the interests and philosophies of the colleges' heads or masters.

Students attend lectures given by professors, usually referred to as dons, and meet regularly with a tutor assigned to them by their own college. They eventually take examinations for different kinds of degrees. Under-graduates may not know the names of all the colleges in the university, but they usually soon learn the names of the most illustrious graduates of their own colleges; often they eat their meals under portraits of their predecessors in the dining hall.

Soon you will be passing the buildings of New College on your left. Enter the gate under the fourteenth-century tower, noticing the oak doors which date from the same period. As you enter the main quadrangle, on your left are the chapel and great hall. Directly ahead of you is the Founder's Library; on the other sides are the rooms or chambers of the Fellows, the teaching and administrating members of the college who elect the head of their house. This design of a four-sided building around a central courtyard originated at New College, but now it has spread around the world as a favourite style for academic architecture.

Although this college was founded as St Mary College of Winchester in 1379, it has always been known as New College. If the college rooms are open, you can explore them; otherwise, go through the arch under the library wing into the garden quad beyond. Have a look at the intricate wrought-iron gates and railings which surround the extensive garden. If you turn to your left you will see parts of the old city wall still standing. As you look at the tranquil green lawns and trees, you may see students sitting on benches in the garden, reading or talking.

Carry on down New College Lane, which curves to become Queen's Lane. This will bring you to Queen's College at the High Street intersection. Although this college, too, was founded in the fourteenth century, its buildings reflect the style of the eighteenth century, for it was largely rebuilt then. Several of the rooms here are worth a visit: the library, one of the most beautiful in Oxford, and Christopher Wren's hall and chapel with its lovely old windows.

Queen's was always a special concern of the Queens Consort of England; Queen Philippa, wife of Edward III, helped to found the college, and a large bequest by Queen Caroline, wife of George II, earned her a statue beneath the gatehouse cupola. The college maintains some ancient and rather idiosyncratic ceremonies: a trumpet announces dinner and at Christmas there is a Boar's Head procession and dinner. At the New Year, each dinner guest is given a needle and thread by the Bursar, who says, 'Take this and be thrifty.'

As you leave Queen's by the High Street gate, turn left toward the bridge over the Cherwell, the small tributary of the Thames River that the Oxonians call the 'Char'. Soon you will see the spires of Magdalen College, which is where you may either finish this walk or begin the next.

Oxford II

> This winter-eve is warm,
> Humid the air! leafless, yet soft as spring,
>   The tender purple spray on copse and briers!
>   And that sweet city with her dreaming spires,
> She needs not June for beauty's heightening.

Matthew Arnold

THE VISITOR'S view of Oxford should take in the lovely surroundings of the colleges that make up the university. This walk invites you to explore some of the parks and garden areas which are dotted among the buildings and which line the river banks.

Almost everyone associates that peculiar activity called 'punting' with Oxford undergraduate pastimes. Start your walk, then, at Magdalen Bridge (always pronounced 'Maudlin' in Oxford). As you look over the stone railings, you will see the small flotilla of narrow wooden shells riding the gentle current of the Cherwell beneath you. Often you will see a punter poling one of the boats downstream alongside the playing fields and meadows. Once, one would have expected to see only men engaged in this ritual, but today one is just as likely to see women punting; no longer do they lounge gracefully in crinolines with their lacy parasols protecting their fair complexions while their male companions do all the work.

In the grounds across the bridge from Magdalen College lies the oldest botanic garden in England, a delightful place

GATE OF THE BOTANICAL GARDENS, OXFORD

to wander for an hour or so. Once the burial ground of the Jews in Oxford, it preserves a quiet charm with its dark cypresses and background of Magdalen's pinnacled towers.

After leaving the garden, turn left and go a few yards back up the High Street until you find Rose Lane, which will lead you to Christ Church Meadow with its tree-bordered walks. Bear right along the edge of the buildings of Merton College, and then right down the lane called 'The Grove' to Merton Street where you will find the tower and gate to the interior quadrangles. Merton is one of the oldest of the Oxford colleges; here you can see the most ancient buildings of the university. They adjoin the oldest courtyard, called 'Mob Quad' though no one knows why. The oldest library in England is here; you can visit it to see the oak reading tables and the shelves which were innovative when they were built in the 1370s. Up to that time, books were stored in presses on their sides instead of upright on their spines.

You will also find a display of Max Beerbohm cartoons. He was a Merton man, as were Thomas Bodley, founder of the university library, Lord Randolph Churchill, Sir Winston's father, and the poet T.S. Eliot.

Retrace your steps along Merton Street and down The Grove, along which are some remnants of the old city wall of Oxford. On your right is Corpus Christi College, with a sundial gracing its rather severe gravelled quad. The pelican on the sundial forms part of the college's coat of arms and the perpetual calendar adds a practical touch. Before the First World War, most of the college quads were covered in gravel or were paved, but now fashion favours the use of grass.

Your next destination is the largest of the colleges, Christ Church, usually referred to simply as 'The House'. Continue skirting the meadow to your right and you will soon see the cathedral on the east side of Tom Quad, the largest quad in Oxford, and Tom Tower on the west side, built by Christopher Wren. Inside the top of the tower is the huge bell (six and a half tons) called 'Great Tom', which peals 101 times at 9.30 each evening to mark the closing of the gates. There were 101 original members of the college foundation. Both Cardinal Wolsey and his king, Henry VIII, supplied funds for the ambitious building project.

Everything at Christ Church seems large, except the cathedral, which is one of the smallest in England. But it is surely one of the most beautiful. The heavy pillars date from the twelfth century, while the delicate vaulting they support is from the fifteenth century. Charles I listened to sermons from the fine carved pulpit when Oxford was his military base during the Civil War. The choir of the cathedral has long been famous; Londoners sometimes journey down to Oxford to hear Evensong here.

It is easy to spend several hours at Christ Church, admiring the buildings, the paintings and memorials to famous graduates, Fellows of the House and clergymen of the cathedral: Dean John Fell (who figures in the verse, 'I do not love thee, Dr Fell/The reason why I cannot tell'); John Locke and William Penn, both of whom were 'sent down' (expelled) for expressing unpopular views; John Wesley; W.E. Gladstone; Edward VII; and the mathematician C.L. Dodgson, a graduate and don of unprepossessing appearance and manner, better known to the world as Lewis Carroll, author of *Alice in Wonderland*. It was on the waters of the River Thames, a mere stream here at the bottom of Christ Church Meadow, that the beloved children's tale was first told by Dogdson to young Alice Liddell and her two sisters as they rowed to a picnic spot.

After looking round the college, you may like to leave through the gate of Tom Tower to St Aldate's. If you prefer a longer ramble, turn left and walk down to Folly Bridge over the Thames, locally known as the Isis River. But if you are ready for a snack and a rest, turn right and you will soon find yourself at the Carfax intersection where St Aldate's becomes Cornmarket. There are numerous shops, pubs and cafés in this busy shopping area.

Before you leave Oxford, however, you should take one more short detour to Pembroke College, where the great Dr Samuel Johnson was a student; a china teapot said to be his is prominently displayed there. There is a narrow path, called Beef Lane, leading to the college along the side of St Aldate's Church across the street from Tom Tower. As you approach the gatehouse, look up at the windows above it. In one of these chambers Johnson lived during the short time he was a university student — tradition has it that he was so poor that one of his classmates secretly took his shoes to be repaired; this good deed so humiliated the proud young man that he left Oxford forthwith. Years later, however, he was awarded an honorary doctorate by the university which was by then glad to acknowledge him as one of its most illustrious students.

The handsome quadrangle and surrounding buildings were built between the seventeenth and nineteenth centuries. The chapel is worth a look, as is the hall. Along the side bordering St Aldate's Church is a row of old alms houses, built by Cardinal Wolsey. The quad has been likened to a small town square because of these examples of domestic architecture.

Among other famous Pembroke members were James Smithson, who later founded the Smithsonian Institution in Washington, DC, and George Whitefield, the Methodist preacher and friend of John Wesley.

As we reach the end of our tour of Oxford, it is important to realize that there is scarcely a place on the globe that has not been touched in important ways by the young men and women who have been educated here. There is not a discipline, an art or a profession which does not number Oxford graduates among its upper echelons, and the touching plaques in many of the halls remind us, too, that many of the students gave up their lives to fight in their country's wars. You may find that Oxford has the power to draw you back to it again and again. And there will be much, much more to see, for we have scarcely scratched the surface of her charms.

Such dusky grandeur clothed the height,
Where the huge castle holds its state,
    And all the steep slope down,
Whose ridgy back heaves to the sky,
Piled deep and massy, close and high,
    Mine own romantic town!

Sir Walter Scott

IT IS Lord Marmion who is surveying the scene described above, but it probably reflects the views of Walter Scott as well, and it accurately reflects the views of many people who have visited Edinburgh. As Alan Bold, a contemporary poet, has written, 'Edinburgh is an experience,' and the experience begins with your first glimpse of that great out-thrust of volcanic rock in the middle of the city, topped by the looming walls of the ancient castle.

As many have pointed out, Edinburgh is an unusual city in that it was not developed beside a river in a fertile plain, but rather grew around this formidable rock. The area long provided a defensible position, of course, and the castle now seems as natural as if it had been thrust up with the rocks themselves.

Yet impregnable as it may seem, the rock has been successfully attacked a number of times. Usually, however, it took guile rather than sheer strength of numbers. One story tells of the time it was taken because one of the men in the attacking force had been stationed there in his youth and

SEVENTEENTH-CENTURY EDINBURGH

knew a secret way down from the rock, which he had used
for the purpose of assignations with local girls when he was
supposed to be on duty. The way down for dalliance proved
equally successful as a way up for attack.

Edinburgh is in many ways two cities — a very old one
that grew gradually larger, in the manner of most cities, and
a new one that was designed in the eighteenth century.
We'll explore both those cities in these two walks: the old
town now and the new town in the next walk. Both hold
great interest for the visitor. Then, as an experienced
walker, you can make further explorations on your own.

Before we begin our walk through the old city, we should
perhaps understand something of the history of Edinburgh.
There was probably a settlement of Picts here even before
the Romans, and after the Romans left, Edwin, King of

Northumbria, rebuilt an old fortress on the rock in the sixth century and the area soon became known as Edwin's Burgh.

During the following centuries, the fortified castle was more or less all that stood in the area, but in the twelfth century a general stability encouraged the development of markets along the spine of the hill leading up to the castle and, at the same time, the establishment of Holyrood Abbey at the foot of the hill. By the early sixteenth century, Edinburgh had become a world centre of art and learning, partly due to generous patronage from the Scottish kings. In the mid-sixteenth century, when Henry VIII of England was unable to get agreement on the marriage of his son to the young Mary Queen of Scots, he attacked and destroyed much of the thriving city. In 1561, Mary returned from France and the stage was set for the ensuing tragedy. We'll discuss this further when we visit Holyrood Palace later on.

In 1603, Mary's son, James VI of Scotland, became James I of England and moved the Scottish court to London. A century later, in 1707, the Act of Union was passed and Scotland ceased to be an independent nation. But although union with England provided economic advantages for Scotland, it was difficult for many Scots to accept the blow to their national pride. Hence it was here, in this disaffected country, that the exiled Stuarts turned for support in their various attempts to regain the throne of England during the eighteenth century. 'Bonnie Prince Charlie', the Young Pretender, actually held court in Holyrood Palace and, after his final defeat at Culloden in 1745, his name became permanently enshrined in Scottish song and folklore.

Finally, in the eighteenth century, Edinburgh developed into something like the city that you will be visiting on these walks. It expanded northwards and the planned areas of wide streets and handsome squares still contain some of the finest Georgian architecture in all of Great Britain. In addition, most heavy industry developed in other cities, notably Glasgow to the west, and so Edinburgh remained the centre of art and culture and education.

In the eighteenth century a great number of brilliant people lived and worked and taught in Edinburgh: David

Hume the historian, Allan Ramsay the poet, Adam Smith the economist, Oliver Goldsmith, Robert Louis Stevenson and Sir Walter Scott. When Dr Johnson accepted James Boswell's invitation to visit Scotland in 1773, it was only partly because of the friendship he felt for Boswell; he was also eager to see Edinburgh and meet with the many intellectuals he knew he would find there.

Anyway, now it is time to begin our walk. Today's expedition will take us along the principal street of the old city. It has a variety of names, but is collectively known as The Royal Mile, because it leads from the old castle at the top to the newer and still used Holyrood Palace at the bottom.

We'll begin at the top, at the castle itself, and work our way down, finishing at Holyrood. The castle is easy to find — it's visible from all over Edinburgh — and since the city began here it seems sensible to begin our walk at this point.

The castle is also easy to reach. It is a steep but not a long walk from the central area of Edinburgh; there are paths up to the Esplanade both from the north and south sides. Public transport and taxis are also available if you require them. One important note: in Scotland, as in England, many public places are closed on Sunday, or open later than usual. Scotland is probably a little more restrictive than England, perhaps because of its Presbyterian heritage. But fortunately Scottish pubs, unlike English ones, are open all day, so you don't have to worry about a place for rest and refreshment.

The tour of the castle begins at the Esplanade, the broad parade ground in front that is the site of the famous military tattoo during the Edinburgh Festival in August each year. There are splendid views of Edinburgh and the surrounding countryside both from the north and south sides of the Esplanade, as there will be later from the castle itself. In the north-east corner you may look for a plaque marking the place where more than three hundred witches were burned, some as late as the eighteenth century. The Scottish Enlightenment was slow in reaching its magistrates.

The castle is entered over the old moat, with statues of two famous Scottish heroes, Bruce and Wallace, on either side. Once inside, the visitor is free to wander at will; you may spend as much time here as you like. One of the buildings you should look for is the tiny St Margaret's Chapel, only large enough for a dozen people to enter at a time. It is the oldest building in Edinburgh and perhaps the oldest complete church building in Britain. It may have been built as early as the eleventh century by Queen Margaret, the wife of Malcolm. Margaret was brought up in Hungary and she was one of the first people to bring continental culture to the young city. Later she achieved sainthood and this small chapel still bears her name.

Mons Meg, the huge cannon that threatens the town of Edinburgh from one of the ramparts, was probably built as early as the fifteenth century and used in a variety of engagements. In the inventory prepared for Cromwell after his soldiers captured the castle, it is described as 'the great iron murderer, Muckle Meg', but the name 'Mons' may come from an old tradition that it was forged near that city in France. In the mid-eighteenth century it was taken to the Tower in London by the English, but through the efforts of Sir Walter Scott it was returned to Edinburgh almost a hundred years later.

The residential quarters at the castle, much rebuilt over the centuries, provide a variety of exhibits, perhaps the most interesting of which are the Scottish royal regalia, including the 'Honours of Scotland', a fine crown, sceptre and sword. Out of fear that they would be taken by the English, they were hidden at the time of the union and then forgotten. In 1818, Sir Walter Scott led the search to the sealed Crown Room where they were found and are now displayed.

Finally, the Scottish National War Memorial lies within the precincts of the castle, as well as the Scottish United Services Museum. The former is a memorial to Scottish soldiers from the First World War; the latter has exhibits of the dress, weapons and equipment of the three armed services — Army, Navy, and Air Force.

Of course there is much more to see and admire at the castle, not least the breathtaking views over the city, but if we are to walk the rest of the Royal Mile it is time to begin.

Today the Royal Mile is filled principally with tourists,

and many of the shops that line the way cater to them, providing lunches, drinks and souvenirs. But in the eighteenth century and earlier, this was the principal thoroughfare of the city, both for living and working, and it was crowded, narrow, noisy and sooty (Old Edinburgh was long called 'Auld Reekie').

Most people lived in crowded flats reached through narrow walkways, called 'wynds', that still exist. You can explore a few of these and get a quick sense of the past. Fortunately, much of old Edinburgh has not really changed: the shop now selling souvenirs perhaps belonged to a cloth merchant two centuries ago and today's expensive restaurant was probably once a busy tavern. But the buildings remain essentially the same and the visitor can get — through the soles of the feet on the cobblestones — a real feeling for the history of these streets.

There are many things to see as you walk along. The Esplanade gives way first to Castle Hill, which in turn will become Lawnmarket — the street of the linen sellers. On the right as you leave the Esplanade is Cannonball House, with a ball embedded in the wall, perhaps fired — rather clumsily — from the castle above at Bonnie Prince Charlie in Holyrood Palace below.

Across the street, on our left, is a tower with a camera obscura which provides, for a fee, fine views of the city below. A little further along, also on our left, is Gladstone's Land, a seventeenth-century building carefully restored, including the shop fronts, and beyond that is James Court, one of the residential areas you might like to explore. David Hume lived here in the eighteenth century and, when Johnson arrived in Edinburgh to meet his friend James Boswell, it was to James Court that he was taken. Whether it was this particular court or not is open to conjecture, for a brass plaque across the street also claims to mark the place where Boswell lived.

A little further down on the left, you will see signs directing you to Lady Stair's House, a remarkably well-preserved seventeenth-century dwelling that is now a museum devoted to three great Scottish writers — Scott, Burns and Stevenson. It is well worth a brief visit.

'MR JOHNSON AND I WALKED ARM IN ARM UP THE
HIGH STREET TO MY HOUSE IN JAMES COURT'

Back on the Royal Mile, the street soon widens to become the High Street and on the right almost at once is Parliament Square and St Giles Cathedral, once the ecclesiastical and political centre of Edinburgh. St Giles has had a confusing history. It was properly a cathedral only for a short time, when Charles I and, after the Restoration, his son, Charles II, established a Bishopric of Edinburgh.

Much earlier, of course, St Giles was the church of the great reformer, John Knox, who was minister here for some twelve years in the mid-sixteenth century, during which time he had some famous debates with Mary Queen of Scots. After the end of the seventeenth century, when the reform movement took hold in Scotland, it ceased to be a cathedral and became simply a church, the High Kirk of

Edinburgh, centre of Scottish Presbyterianism.

A church has stood on this spot probably since the ninth century, but the present structure dates from the fifteenth, although so much of it has been rebuilt that it is hardly recognizable as a medieval church. Its most notable feature remains the old tower, with the unique Crown of St Giles on top. The church is worth a visit for the many monuments and records to be found inside.

The south side of Parliament Square is occupied by Parliament House, where the Scottish parliament met until it was dissolved in 1707. It is presently still used as government offices and as courtrooms. In the courtyard is an equestrian statue of Charles II and, a little further west, a heart-shaped design in the stone of the courtyard marks the location of the old Tolbooth, the notorious prison which Scott dramatized in the opening scenes of his novel, *Heart of Midlothian*. When the prison was torn down in 1817, Scott rescued the door through which prisoners walked to their execution, along with the massive keys; they are still on display at Abbotsford, Scott's home, now a museum.

One other note: John Knox's grave is supposed to be here, since Parliament Square covered up an old grave-yard. It is ironically appropriate, if so, because Samuel Johnson, who hated the anti-establishment views of John Knox, wished at one time that he might be buried in a highway; now the square is chiefly used as a car park.

The ghost of John Knox continues to haunt us on this walk, for, a little further on, jutting out into the High Street so that you can't miss it is John Knox's House. Whether or not Knox actually lived and died there is debatable, but the house itself is a remarkable example of late fifteenth-century construction and is well worth a visit.

Inside, there are some fine wood panelling, narrow staircases and low-ceilinged rooms. Here you can find pamphlets and other material about Knox. Four hundred years after his death, a final judgement about him has still not been made. By some he is seen as a narrow-minded, Puritanical reformer who was responsible for the rigorous Sabbath and distrust of popular amusements that still seem to dominate some areas of Scotland; by others he is looked upon as a social and political reformer who brought his influence to bear against the unjust power of an absolute monarchy and the excesses of Roman Catholicism.

The literature available here will give you insight into many aspects of his fascinating character, as well as providing information about the dramatic confrontation between him and the teenaged, widowed Mary Queen of Scots. Not only were their principles opposed, but their very natures seemed antithetical: the dour, elderly minister who had served a year as a galley slave and been buffeted all over Europe and the British Isles by the winds of the Reformation, and the witty young queen who had been brought up in the midst of all the glitter and opulence of the European courts. Mary eventually was executed, and Knox died in his bed, perhaps in this very house, but their ghosts haunt our steps throughout this Royal Mile.

Almost across the street from the John Knox House is the Museum of Childhood, not so much a museum for children, but rather more a place for adults to relive their own childhoods. In addition to displaying a remarkable collection of old toys and dolls and children's clothes, there are full-scale figures representing childhood in the past — for example there is a nineteenth-century grammar school, with the master standing in front holding a pointer and the blackboard full of difficult fractions. Wonderful souvenirs are for sale as well — colouring books, cardboard cut-outs, old-fashioned toys and dolls.

Almost every building you pass on the Royal Mile has its historic associations, but we shall stop at only two more places on our way to Holyrood. First, on the right-hand side, comes the City Museum, Huntly House. The exhibits here provide a history of Edinburgh from its earliest beginnings to the present day. The artefacts are more simply displayed than those at the Museum of London in the Barbican (see Walk No. 10). It is easy to spend a lot of time in Huntly House, for there are many rooms and much to see; you may wish to return another day.

Back on the left side of the street, and nearly at the bottom, you will find White Horse Close. By now the street is called Canongate and Holyrood can be seen ahead. White

Horse Close is interesting because it was here that Samuel Johnson came when he first arrived in Edinburgh and it was from here that he sent a message to Boswell saying that he had arrived. Afterwards, when Boswell came to fetch him, the two walked arm in arm together up to Boswell's house near the top of the hill — keeping to the middle of the narrow street, in order to avoid unwanted deposits from the upstairs windows. A marvellous contemporary print shows the two friends making this journey. White Horse Close has been much rebuilt over two centuries, but eighteenth-century prints of the inn that stood here show that the street still looks much the same now as then.

Finally, at the end of the Royal Mile stands Holyrood Abbey and the Palace of Holyroodhouse. The Abbey is much the older of the two buildings, perhaps begun as early as the twelfth century. The name means Holy Cross and one legend suggests that it comes from a piece of the True Cross that was supposed to have been in the possession of Queen Margaret who founded the Abbey. There is another story that the king, out hunting on this spot, was about to be gored by a stag, but was saved by the appearance of a cross.

The Abbey was certainly a splendid structure, used as a residence by many of the Scottish kings in the fourteenth and fifteenth centuries because it was far more comfortable than the draughty castle up the hill. It was rebuilt many times and later destroyed during the Reformation, then partly rebuilt later by the English kings Charles I and Charles II. Its unfortunate present condition is the result of the roof collapsing in the late eighteenth century because repairs had been improperly made.

Today, the Palace is still the official residence of the English monarch when visiting Scotland; when the Queen is here it is not open to the public. But the rest of the time there are tours which take a little less than an hour by a knowledgeable guide who points out all the historical sites, including the spot where the Italian Rizzio was murdered while the pregnant Queen Mary, his friend and possibly his lover, was forced to watch.

The fascinating story of Mary Queen of Scots can hardly be told here in any detail, but a brief summary will help the visitor appreciate the unhappy life of the young queen.

Married very young to the heir of the French throne, Mary spent her early years in France, where she became converted to Roman Catholicism and experienced the gaiety of the French court. When her husband died very young, the eighteen-year-old Mary was hardly prepared for queenship in her own rather dour, puritanical country.

She returned to Holyrood with her priests and courtiers in her entourage and found herself in the middle of Scotland's Reformation, confronted almost at once by the figurehead of that movement, the rigid, strait-laced John Knox. Perhaps partly out of desperation, she married Lord Darnley.

Darnley conspired in the murder of Mary's favourite, friend and 'secretary', Rizzio, with the support or at least acquiescence of John Knox, who felt that Rizzio was a bad influence on the young queen. But shortly after, Mary herself conspired in the murder of her husband, and eight weeks later made another impetuous marriage to her co-conspirator, Lord Bothwell.

After her son by Lord Darnley was born, Mary was imprisoned by the Scots on account of her apparently outrageous behaviour and because she persisted in her Catholicism. She managed to flee to England, hoping to gain support from her Protestant cousin, Queen Elizabeth. Instead, Elizabeth had her imprisoned and finally executed in the Tower.

Was Mary, Queen of Scots, a poor innocent, manipulated girl who never had a chance, or was she a conniving, wicked queen who deserved her fate? Even after five hundred years it is hard to make a final judgement, but it is difficult not to feel sympathy for the teenager who loved to dance and longed for love, thrust into the self-serving political and ecclesiastical arena of fifteenth-century Scotland. The rooms of Holyrood Palace are haunted by the presence of the young queen, and the visitor will re-live her story in walking through them.

After Holyrood, the walk is completed. In the next expedition, we will explore that other part of the city, with its more recent but no less fascinating history.

> Even thus, methinks, a city reared should be,
> > Yea, an imperial city . . . highest in arts enroll'd,
> Highest in arms; brave tenement for the free,
> > Who never crouch to thrones, or sin for gold.

Arthur Henry Hallam

THESE LINES are part of a sonnet entitled 'Edinburgh', written by a nineteenth-century Englishman, a young man whose untimely death at the age of twenty-two inspired his friend, Lord Tennyson, to produce one of his best long poems, *In Memoriam*. Hallam's vision of Edinburgh shows the kind of respect the English have for their northern neighbours, whose fierce pride and independence — even after the formal union with England — remain as strong as ever. Further, Hallam calls Edinburgh 'an imperial city', and he is thinking, surely, not only of the old town we have visited in our first walk, with its ancient castle and ruined abbey, but of the new town that had just been built on the level land to the north, which provided people in the early nineteenth century with a model of what a modern, planned community could be.

It is the new town that we will examine today. It has aged well and, even though there are hamburger stands and souvenir shops scattered among its monuments, it remains a dignified, stately part of the city, with broad avenues, dignified squares and handsome Georgian buildings.

211

Our walk today will follow an irregular circle, beginning at the west end of Princes Street, moving northward into the new town and then westward to St Andrew Square, back to Princes Street with a glance up Calton Hill, and finally down Princes Street, or through the parallel gardens, to where we began. But this walk must be considered only as an introduction to all that Edinburgh has to offer; it is intended principally as orientation to your own later exploration.

New Town was begun in the late eighteenth century, and building continued well into the nineteenth. The basic plan, as a look at any city map will show, was quite straightforward and extremely regular. The principal east–west boulevard is George Street, running along the ridge and named after George III. Parallel to the north runs Queen Street and, to the south, Princes Street, named after the Prince of Wales, whom we met earlier as 'Prinny' (see Walks No. 15 and 19).

In addition, the deep valley between Princes Street and Castle Hill, which had been a watery loch, was filled in and designed as a linear garden. All of these plans were originally devised by a young architect named James Craig and carried out over the years by many different people, but always with a remarkable unity of design and purpose.

Princes Street, of course, has become Edinburgh's principal street; the north side offers a variety of shops and hotels and restaurants. Queen Street and George Street, as well as the major cross streets, are still primarily residential or professional, with several important public buildings and churches.

We'll begin at the west end of Princes Street, a major intersection. On the corner to the south is St John's Church and, not far behind, St Cuthbert's. Both are nineteenth-century buildings, although St Cuthbert's is built on a very old foundation and its tower was built in 1789. These churches seem dark and rather gloomy, even oppressive, compared with the clear windows and bright colours of the Wren churches we visited in London (Walk No. 13); the appearance may reflect some of the doctrinal differences between the Presbyterian Church of Scotland and eighteenth-century English Anglicanism.

212

We'll start our walk north-west from this busy intersection along Queensferry Street. As the name suggests, this road originally led to the ferry; now it will take you to the Forth Bridge. But we'll walk only a very short distance, to Randolph Crescent, one of the beautifully designed Georgian residential areas and the first of three such areas set in a northeasterly row. The second is Ainslie Place, a kind of shallow oval, followed by Moray Place, a complete circle.

You may walk up to Moray Place if you wish, but we will leave this area at the south-east corner of Ainslie Place, down Hope Street as far as Charlotte Square, which is really the western vestibule to the splendid rectangle of New Town's principal boulevards.

Charlotte Square was one of the last designs of Robert Adam; in fact, he died before it was completed. The north side has a particularly striking series of façades, most of which now belong to the National Trust of Scotland. The lower floors of No. 7 are furnished in the style of a typical late eighteenth-century, early nineteenth-century house; they are open to visitors.

From Charlotte Square, George Street east to St Andrew Square is a little more than half a mile. It is a beautiful street to walk along, with many fine public buildings and a number of plaques which indicate the famous people who have lived here.

Still, you may like to make the trip eastward via a more zigzag route. To the north, Queen Street is almost equally grand and is bordered by Queen Street Gardens. And at some point you should walk along the narrow Rose Street, paralleling George Street to the south, between George Street and Princes Street.

Rose Street is a different experience from the elegant George Street. There are small shops, pubs and restaurants, and usually far more people than you will see walking along George Street. Many of the restaurants offer ethnic menus and you may like to examine some with a view to returning for lunch or dinner.

Finally, back on George Street, just before St Andrew Square, to the north, you will pass St Andrew's Church, built in the late eighteenth century, the first church to be built in New Town.

At St Andrew Square, turn left or north into Queen Street and on your right you will find the Scottish National Portrait Gallery and the National Museum of Antiquities, both in the same building. The Portrait Gallery, like its English counterpart in London, dramatizes Scottish history by displaying drawings and portraits of the principal players.

The National Museum of Antiquities offers the visitor a multitude of exhibits relating to Scottish history, from prehistoric times to the present, including many domestic artefacts that help to illustrate the lives of ordinary people throughout the centuries. Both these places deserve an extended visit; today if you decide to stay some time you might consider postponing the balance of this walk for another day.

But when you decide to carry on, walk south along the east side of St Andrew Square, down St Andrew Street, to Princes Street once more, We will eventually turn right to return to our starting point, but first we will look around to see what this neighbourhood has to offer.

To the left, Princes Street soon becomes Waterloo Place and curves south towards the Palace of Holyroodhouse, around Calton Hill, one of the highest points in Edinburgh apart from Castle Hill. On top you can get a glimpse of the unfinished Parthenon, the National Monument to honour the dead in the Napoleonic Wars, begun in the early nineteenth century. Also on the hill is the Nelson Monument, which you can climb for an excellent view of the city and surrounding countryside, and the City Observatory. You can get up the hill by climbing the public steps at the place where Waterloo Place becomes Regent Road, or follow a road up further along.

Also at the eastern end of Princes Street is the General Post Office and, to the south, the Waverley Railway Station. Across Waterloo Place from the Post Office is Register House, where most important public records are kept and, behind that, the modern group of restaurants, shops, offices and hotels known as the St James Centre. But now we will turn back to Princes Street and the gardens, and gradually return to our starting point, with a number of stops along the way.

There are two possible routes to follow from here: if you are an inveterate window-shopper you will wish to stay on the north side of Princes Street and browse your way slowly westward. Here you will find Scottish tartans, shortbreads and other good things to eat, fine clothing and jewellery shops, souvenir stands and restaurants. Alternatively, you may prefer to head south at the first opportunity and work your way west through the peaceful and colourful gardens. We will describe chiefly the things that are to be found in the gardens and leave the shops to the shoppers.

The most striking monument of Princes Street is right before us — the amazing Gothic monument to Sir Walter Scott. The spire is two hundred feet high and beneath the canopy stands a statue of Scott with his dog. If you like, you can climb the monument for a fine view of Princes Street and the gardens.

Just before the monument, Waverley Bridge leads south in a curving route to the old town, past the Tourist Information and Accommodation Centre. This may be a good place to visit when you are planning future explorations of Edinburgh, for they can provide you with maps and other useful materials. Like other Tourist Information Centres, they will also help you find a place to stay, either in a hotel or in a private home that offers 'Bed and Breakfast' accommodation.

The Scott Monument stands in the East Princes Street Gardens, which are divided from the West Gardens by The Mound, one of the principal streets leading up to the Esplanade. The Mound also contains two of Scotland's most important art galleries, the Royal Scottish Academy, closest to Princes Street, and the National Gallery of Scotland, a little further along. The Royal Scottish Academy usually has several special exhibitions each summer; the National Gallery includes an important collection of European painting, with a special emphasis on Scottish artists. Both these galleries deserve an extended visit, but there is hardly time on this orientation walk.

From The Mound, you can work your way eastward through the Princes Street Gardens by a number of paths. South, on the slope of Castle Hill, is a path that provides a pleasant view of the gardens below. Or you can take one of several paths nearer to Princes Street and perhaps note the interesting Floral Clock in the corner of Princes Street and The Mound. Built in 1903, this may be the oldest floral clock in the world; it is surely one of the most impressive, with a variety of arrangements at different times of the year.

About halfway down the gardens towards our starting point you will pass the Ross Open Air Theatre, where there is regular entertainment during the summer. It is a good place to see traditional Scottish dancing or to hear the music of the bagpipe.

Still further along is the American War Memorial; by then you will be in sight of the two churches that marked the beginning of our walk and the path that will lead you back to Princes Street. On Princes Street and behind, on the narrow Rose Street, there are plenty of places to stop for a cup of tea or coffee or something stronger.

*

This is the last of this series of walks and by now, having completed a number of them, the apprentice walker should have become a journeyman or journeywoman, perhaps well on the way to becoming a master walker and joining the illustrious company of walkers to whom this book is dedicated. If these walks have succeeded in whetting your appetite for more, if an unexplored street now proves an irresistible lure, if every new town or city you enter makes you want to put on your walking shoes and get started — then this book has succeeded in its aim and we can say, with John Gay in the last line of his long poem: 'This Work shall shine, and Walkers bless our Name.'